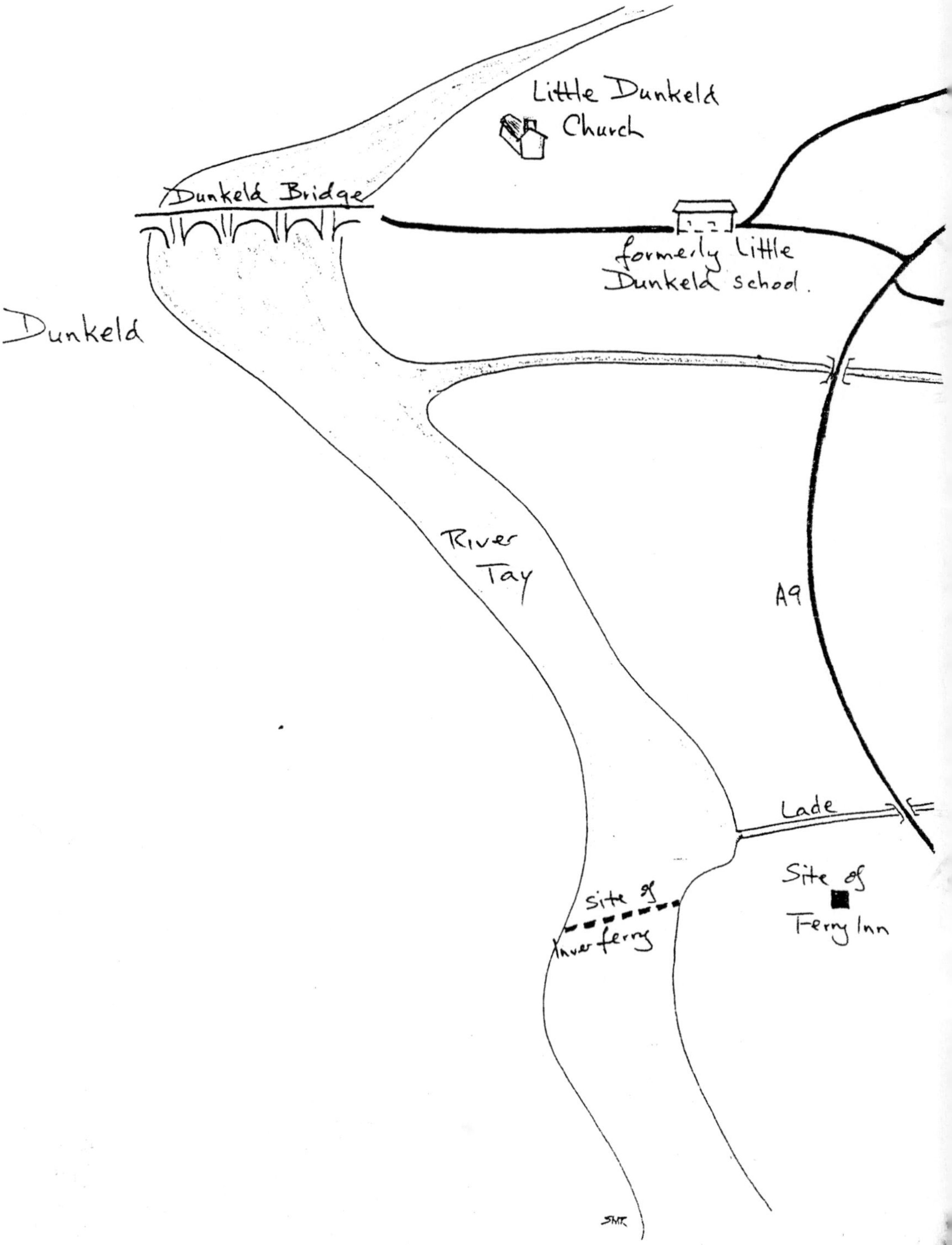

Little Dunkeld
Church

Dunkeld Bridge

Dunkeld

formerly Little
Dunkeld school.

River
Tay

A9

Lade

Site of
Ferry Inn

Site of
Inver ferry

SMK

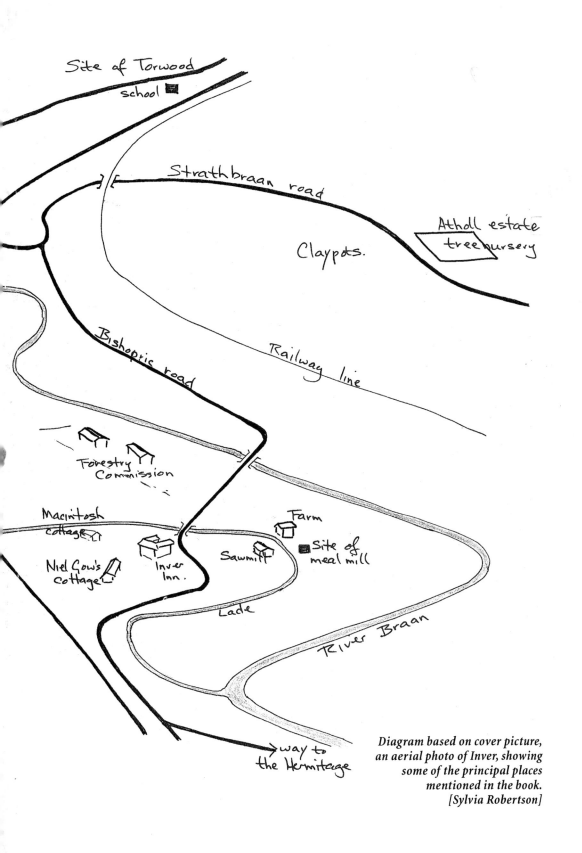

Site of Torwood school

Strathbraan road

Atholl estate tree nursery

Claypots.

Bishopric road

Railway line

Forestry Commission

Macintosh cottage

Niel Gow's cottage

Inver Inn.

Sawmill

Farm

Site of meal mill

Lade

River Braan

way to the Hermitage

Diagram based on cover picture, an aerial photo of Inver, showing some of the principal places mentioned in the book.
[Sylvia Robertson]

The road as you enter the village of Inver. [S Robertson]

Niel Gow's Inver

Helen Jackson

Perth & Kinross Libraries

Cover: *Aerial view of Inver. [Alison Brydon]*

To Doctor Roger Leitch without whose help and encouragement
this book would not have been written.

The Publisher is grateful for financial assistance from the Keepers of the Quaich toward the publication costs of this book.

ISBN 0 905452 30 5

Published by
Perth & Kinross Libraries
AK Bell Library
York Place
Perth
PH2 8EP

PERTH &
KINROSS
COUNCIL

The publisher also thanks Dunkeld & Birnam Historical Society for their financial assistance

Printed by
Cordfall Ltd
0141 572 0878

Contents

Inver—the village and its people

The Author

It was inevitable that Helen Jackson should publish the contents of this book one day—though the writing and preparation for it has taken a lifetime—a lifetime steeped in the parish of Little Dunkeld, in the village of Inver and in the lives of the people who lived there. Her early mentor, guide and friend was her Aunt Kate (Jackson) who lived in Hillside Cottage, Birnam and with whom Helen spent childhood holidays. She remembers that the old and somewhat tuneless piano was always adorned with Niel Gow's music. His name and that of Charlie Macintosh were, Helen says, household words. The diversions for the young Helen were walks to Torwood, up Birnam Hill and, most importantly, to Inver. Those guided tours were the background of the future researches—the cottages, the River Braan, the lades filled by the river and the mills which the water powered. All was later to slip into place when the serious work began—but that was not until her professional life was over and increased leisure would allow her to delve into the archives of Register House, the National Library, Blair Castle and the AK Bell Library in Perth. In this book lies the fulfilment of these endeavours.

Acknowledgements

Numerous individuals from varied walks of life have helped bring *Niel Gow's Inver* to fruition since I first embarked on the project in the early 1980s.

Firstly I wish to extend my deepest gratitude to the Keepers of the Quaich for providing financial assistance towards the production costs of this book. Over a period of years spent sifting through the Atholl archives at Blair Castle I received unstinted co-operation and friendly advice from the archivist Mrs Jane Anderson who also went out of her way to explore this treasure trove of source materials on my behalf. Mrs Eileen Cox of the Dunkeld and Birnam Historical Society kindly undertook proofreading and revision as well as compiling the index. From my barely legible pencil manuscript, Mrs Sylvia Robertson had the unenviable task of providing typescript and also assisted in checking certain sources.

Foremost among the number of institutions I consulted was the AK Bell Library in Perth and I would especially like to acknowledge the friendly services of Mr Jeremy Duncan, Mr Stephen Connolly, Mrs Lorna Mitchell and Mr Iain MacRae who each helped out in their ubiquitous and efficient way. The staffs at the National Library of Scotland and the Scottish Record Office in Edinburgh lessened the burden of searching their vast resources by courteous and knowledgable guidance, as well as dealing with numerous telephone requests to suggest possible sources.

I had the good fortune to find in Mr Iain Scott from High Wycombe an adept and avidly keen genealogist who utilised his computer skills to produce the Gow family tree—which can be viewed in full on Perth & Kinross Library's web site, www.pkc.gov.uk,—and provided a great many points of interest in connection with the Gow family world wide.

Last, but by no means least, I wish to extend my warmest gratitude to the people of Inver and in particular to Mrs Erica Lyon, the present occupier of the cottage where Niel Gow lived all his life.

Footnote / Illustration Abbreviations

A.A.   Atholl Archives
O.S.A. Old Statistical Accounts
N.L.S. National Library of Scotland
H.S.L. Highland Society of London
G.U.S. Glasgow University Library.
H.J.   Helen Jackson

Foreword

I have always felt fortunate being able to grow up and live in rural Perthshire, Scotland, in the place where my father and grandfather lived and worked. I feel fortunate also—being a composer and fiddle player myself—that this is where Niel Gow, often called 'The Father of Scottish Fiddle Music' lived and created.

I first became aware of Niel Gow's music through school friends of mine who lived in Niel Gow's cottage in Inver near Dunkeld. From then till now his hauntingly beautiful airs, stately strathspeys and earthy, rhythmic jigs and reels have been an inspiration to me and a joy to play.

The music of Niel Gow stems from the very heart of the man, as well as his relationship with the community and the land that surrounded him. This book will shed further light on Niel Gow and will be welcomed by the increasing number of his 'enthusiasts' all over the world.

Dougie MacLean

An old print of Niel Gow's cottage

Niel Gow

and the musical heritage of Inver

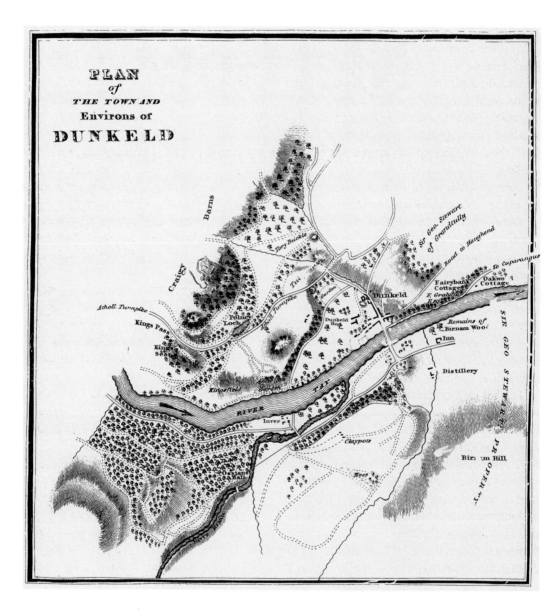

Map by J. Wood, 1823, showing Inver and Claypots. [HJ]

Niel Gow—the man

The name of Niel Gow and Inver have been inextricably linked in the minds of musicians for generations down to the present day, yet, as far as we can judge from the rentals, the Gow family lived there for less than a hundred years, a short sojourn compared to some other families.

Nathaniel, his son, stated that Niel was born in 1727 in Strathbraan. This was later contradicted by Joseph McGregor who scored out Strathbraan in his manuscript account and substituted Inver. The distinction is important. The parish of Little Dunkeld is sharply divided into Highland and Lowland areas. Strathbraan lies in the Highlands, while the village of Inver is Lowland. As late as 1891, the census record for that year shows Strathbraan almost entirely Gaelic speaking, while any Gaelic speakers in Inver had not been born there. This would mean that Niel was Gaelic speaking in his early years, before he went to school. It also explains his Highland dress, his strong devotion to his native place and his family, but above all the character of much of his composition.

Joseph McGregor also suggests that Niel was the first of his family to show musical ability. Alison Kinnaird, in her informative book *The Tree of Strings*, puts forward another view. She suggests that Niel was descended from a long line of McEwan harpers through his mother, Catherine McEwan, a more likely conclusion.

Less than a mile above Inver, in the area of Ladywell, lay the settlement of Claypots. One of the small farms there in 1754 was held jointly by tack by the families of Gow and McEwan. I suggest that this was Niel's birthplace, but it is speculation. McGregor, and subsequent biographers who have accepted his account, stated that John Gow was a plaid weaver. No doubt he wove the wool that his wife had spun on her muckle wheel, as so many of the Strathbraan farmers did, for their own domestic use, but it is unlikely that he ever did so for a living.

Further up Strathbraan, just across the hill from Claypots, lay the hamlet of Tomgarrow, where two families of Cameron had small holdings. Tomgarrow was owned by the Stewarts of Grantully. Could this be where Niel's teacher, John Cameron, lived? Again speculation. Hard facts are hard to come by as the Little Dunkeld Parish Records were partially destroyed during the Militia Riots of 1797. Further church and parish records have been lost or destroyed at a later date.

Niel's skill came to the notice of a wider public when he won a competition for fiddle playing held in Perth around 1744. Later that year, Niel played in a band which entertained Prince Charles at Dunkeld House, where the Young Pretender had a brief stay on his way to Perth. It is said by some that Niel followed the Prince as far as Luncarty, but I doubt it. The district was deeply divided between loyalty to the exiled William, Duke of Atholl and their present laird Duke James his younger brother, for whom Donald Gow, Niel's younger brother, was acting as a messenger.

Niel married Margaret Wiseman, possibly around 1750, for William their eldest child was born in 1751. The stone rubble, broom thatched cottage which he held without a tack was to be his home for the next fifty seven years. At first, the rental was partly in kind, 3 poultry and 3 days darg in addition to £2 6s. Scots per annum. [1] At that time, John and Andrew Gow, possibly Niel's brothers, were established as smiths in Inver, John as a liferenter and Andrew having a tack of a house.

There Niel carried on his trade as a hand loom linen weaver, as most other cottars in the village did. In addition, he cultivated his acre of land, grew vegetables in his kail yard, milked his cows and

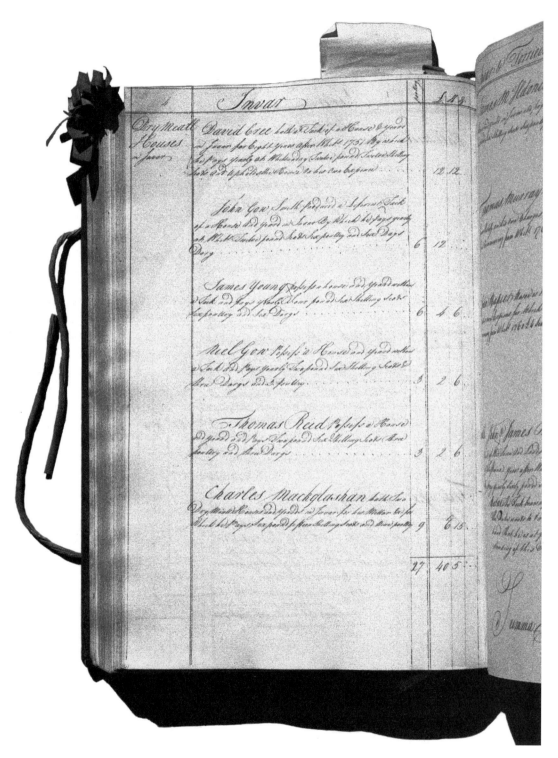

Entry from rent book 1754. [AA 7/418]

played his fiddle, thus providing for his ever growing family. John was born in 1753, Andrew about 1756, Margaret in 1759, Grizel 1761, Nathaniel 1763 and Daniel 1765.

Around 1766 Margaret died, no doubt exhausted by continuous child bearing. Niel, left with a young family, did what so many widowers have done before and since, very sensibly, looked for another wife. His choice fell on another Margaret, of the family of Urchart in Perth. The banns were cried and they were married in 1768. She brought him great happiness for thirty years and proved a loving mother to his children, for she had none of her own.

By this time Niel was being paid £5 per annum as a retainer by the 3rd. Duke of Atholl for playing at family entertainments. [2] In 1766 he was paid for teaching fiddle to the young John Crerar, the Duke's gamekeeper. His older children were also being taught on a kit fiddle, all three showing promise. It was a very busy life, a hard life even, but financially quite comfortable. Weavers were paid rather better than the average tradesman, especially when trade was good. There was a slack time between August and the end of November when the flax crop was being harvested. This allowed Niel to attend the gathering in of the oats and barley on his own acre of land and lift the potatoes and turnips in his kail-yard.

The older children from the age of eight or nine would be expected to do their bit, such as keeping the cattle from straying onto the crops, bringing the cow home for milking, perhaps making an extra penny or two helping with the horses at the inn, or joining the other lads bringing down the peats from Birnam Hill. Margaret would be expected to help her mother with the household chores, taking her share of looking after the younger children, feeding the hens, gathering in the eggs, while her mother milked the cow and churned the butter. Yes, spring and summer were times of great activity, much of it communal, and happy, always providing the weather was good.

The winter days were for school, spinning, weaving and for the children the tiresome chore of winding the yarn onto the bobbins. Once the work was done it was time for music making, dancing in the barn and yarning round the fireside.

Despite having so many mouths to feed, Niel was able to put away a tidy sum of money. His rent was no longer in kind and in Scots money, but £1 10s. sterling per annum for the house and the same for the land. The Gows showed two distinctly different abilities in managing money. Niel, along with his sons John and Andrew, were shrewd men. William and Nathaniel were not so. Andrew Gow, the Inver blacksmith, finding himself in financial difficulties in 1762, turned to Niel for help. In 1767 his wife Elspeth Ealdge pledged property in Dunkeld, which she had inherited from her grandfather, to Niel as security for a bond. Niel finally acquired the property, known as Castle Clearach, which was in poor condition. He rebuilt it, reselling it in 1775. The records in the Scottish Record Office show Niel lending money through the issuing of a bond, a common way of raising a loan before the setting up of local banks. It does render the anecdote about Niel being short of cash and borrowing from Abercairny for instance, seem a bit ridiculous.

Niel had dispensed with his loom, which would have taken up so much space in the kitchen. His way of life was slowly changing. With the older boys growing into manhood, thought had to be given to their future, which seemed to Niel not to lie in Inver. Like so many Little Dunkeld parents,

Niel Gow's signature 1779. [AA 5/141]

he wanted a better future for his family and that seemed to lie in Edinburgh. He was well aware that his sons had great talent and desired a classical music education for them. It is highly likely that they had flown the nest by the end of the 1770s. More of their careers will be told in a later section.

Meantime, Niel was by now leading the life of a professional musician as well as attending to his croft. We get glimpses of him in various letters of the Atholl family.

Charlotte Murray to her brother Captain George Murray. Dunkeld September 1771, 'The children went out walking and brought home Niel Gow with them, as all the servants were resolved on a dance, as they could not get it the day before'. [3]

Diary of Mary Murray, daughter of Lord John Murray. London 1 September 1779:

> In the evening we had Niel Gow the famous Scotch player on the fiddle, who played several tunes. The Maddens sung again and the Scotch fiddler played Donald and other tunes. I went to General Robertsons. After tea, Miss Robertson played. Then the Scotch fiddler appeared. I danced a reel with Miss Murray, Lord Drummond and Captain Murray. [4]

A letter from the Duchess of Atholl to her sister, Mary Graham, describes the celebration at Dunkeld on 30 June 1783 to mark the Duke's birthday:

> They lasted from one o'clock, when the guns were fired, until four o'clock the following morning when daylight had taken the place of candlelight. A company of fifty six were served dinner in a large tent on the lawn while the work people were served theirs in the Avenue before the house. Tea was then served for the Ladies and Gentlemen in the Drawing room.
>
> During that time we were amused with seeing the workmen etc. dance before the Windows. After Tea we returned to the Tents and the Company began dancing upon the Green ... the whole Town and environs of Dunkeld turned out to see the sport. When darkness fell a bonfire was lit on the river following which the people in Dunkeld set off fireworks and several houses in the town were illuminated. After supper there was singing, followed by dancing. Niel Gow and his Brother played incessantly for upwards 12 hours. [5]

This description indicates how Niel Gow earned his annual fee as well as showing his and his brother Donald's stamina. It also illustrates the Highland informality with which the Atholls shared their pleasure with their friends, their servants and the Dunkeld people.

Christmas was another time of jollification at Dunkeld, as the Duchess related to her sister Mary in 1784:

> We had Niel Gow, and when the Desert was set down the Dining-room door opened and Bacchus appeared sitting upon his Casks with a Silver Flask in his hands, He was drawn in triumph round the table by Cupid and Harlequin and Columbine ... after Tea the same Party came into the Drawing-room and shewed themselves to great advantage to the sound of Niel Gow's Fiddle. A March was then played and Charlotte, her Brother and John, joined Harlequin, Columbine and Bacchus in Marching round the room, Cupid following by himself, then they formed into their sixsome Reel which looked very

pretty, and afterwards all danced separately their Hornpipes and then Minuets, Strathspeys, Reels etc.....Afterwards the company danced till Supper, after which began the singing. [6]

These letters illustrate the gusto with which the Atholls enjoyed themselves with Niel more than willing to join in the fun. It also explains the familiarity which at times Niel showed towards the Atholls, and which so surprised and even shocked those un-acquainted with the easy relationship that existed between the Highland laird and his followers. This will be discussed more fully later.

By this time, of course, Niel's fame had spread to other country houses as the old laird of Strowan, writing to his grand-daughter at Gask in 1778, illustrates:

> I am curious to hear Niel Gow that you commend so much, that I might compare him with Kennedy and old Cattanach who were the best hands at country music that I ever heard.... You say that the Minuet is wearing out of fashion, which is a mark of bad taste in dancing. [7]

Niel was invited to play at Orchil but snow prevented him from making the long journey, much to the disappointment of Margaret Oliphant, a guest:

> Niel Gow, a famous Highland fiddler, having been appointed to be at Orchill last month, I was asked there in hopes of having a fine dance, and Niel ran in my head for several days. Well away I went but no Niel today, well tomorrow will bring him.... At last comes music at supper the second day, but alas! it was a scraper ... however the spirit moved us and away with tables chairs and carpets in a moment.... [8]

The 1780s was a busy, productive period for Niel. By this time all the family had flown the nest. It is presumed that the youngest son, Daniel, and younger daughter, Grizel, died in infancy as nothing more is ever heard of them. Margaret, the elder daughter, went to Edinburgh, perhaps to keep house for her brothers initially, but in 1787 she married James MacDonald a dancing master there.

As well as Niel's commitments to the Atholl family, he also fulfilled engagements further afield at hunt balls in Cupar and Perth, or taking the road though the Sma' Glen to the west, there to entertain at Abercairney, Auchtertyre and Crieff. To all these venues he travelled on foot, carrying his fiddle in a green bag on his back, as was the custom with fiddlers at that time. He could have afforded to travel on horseback for by this time he was comfortably off, but he preferred to use shanks' pony. He must have been a very fit man. It seems that it was not unusual in Little Dunkeld, that those who survived the perils of childhood were sturdy, living to a ripe old age. The *Statistical Accounts* [9] and later census records show evidence of this, the most famous being John Stiel, a Blue Coat (travelling beggar) who lived to the age of 105!

Niel, like other fiddlers, shepherds and smugglers, was well acquainted with the many tracks through the hills taking the most direct route to his destinations. No doubt there were many farmhouses and shepherds cottages on the way where his cheery presence would be welcomed by people living in isolation. He was also offered shelter on his journey in the country houses. For instance, when travelling to Aberdeen he was made welcome at Brechin Castle, the home of the Earl of Dalhousie, a faithful patron to Niel and later to his son Nathaniel.

Finally, when he was in his 70s, his legs gave out, as he relates in a letter to Nathaniel in March 1802, '...I think that I never will be in Edinburgh again ther is on my Leges Sweld very much that I am not able to go anywhere with it ...'[10]

Niel's travels were at an end. However, when he was at home there was a steady stream of visitors eager to hear him play either at his cottage or at the inns at Inver and Dunkeld. The stone where he liked to sit, observing the many visitors passing on their way to the Hermitage, is still to be seen outside his cottage.

Of all the visitors who made their way to the Gow cottage, the most memorable was Robert Burns. In August 1787 the poet, along with his friend Nicoll, a schoolmaster, set off from Edinburgh in a post chaise on a tour of the Highlands. Unfortunately, the diary that Burns kept on his journey is tantalisingly brief and disjointed, making it hard to piece together his choice of route. His notes for Thursday 30 August state:

> Come down Tay to Dunkeld—Glenlyon House—Lyon River—Druids Temple—three circles of stones, the outermost sunk; the second has thirteen stones remaining, the innermost has eight; two large detached ones like a gate, to the south-east.—Say prayers in it—Pass Tay Bridge—Aberfeldy—described in rhyme—Castle Menzies, beyond Grandtully—Ballechin—Logierait—Inver—Dr Stewart—Sup.

And on Friday 31 August, 'Walk with Mrs Stewart and Beard to Birnam top—fine prospect down Tay—Craigie Barns Hills—Hermitage and Bran [sic] water with a picture of Ossian—Breakfast with Dr Stewart'.[11]

Niel Gow's cottage in Inver. [HJ]

Who was Beard? I assume that it was the Reverend George Baird, a friend of Burns, who was ordained minister of Dunkeld Cathedral in 1786; he also acted as tutor to the Atholl family and later became Principal of Edinburgh University. Nathaniel Gow states that it was Principal Baird who wrote Niel's memoir in the *Scot's Magazine* in 1809.

Their most direct route to Birnam Hill that morning would be to cross the Tay at the East Ferry and proceed up Birnam Glen. Once at the top, the view over to Craigiebarns and southwards down the Tay would indeed be glorious, as it is today. To continue their journey, they would then cross the Inchewan Burn at the Green Ford and find the track used by the Inver herd boys through Ladywell, making their way to the Hermitage and Ossian's Hall. From there they would join the old Strathbraan road leading to the West Ferry, arriving back at the Stewart's home with sharpened appetites, ready for a late breakfast. This interpretation of Burn's notes contradicts Alex Murdoch's version in his publication *The Fiddle in Scotland* where he writes:

> While attending to his exacting professional duties, the doctor's worthy wife proved an excellent substitute for her husband and led the poet and his friend through the ancient cathedral, to the top of Birnam Hill on the south side of the river, and to Craigie Barns on the north. On the return of the party to Dunkeld Dr Stewart was at liberty to spend the afternoon and evening with his friends.... [12]

No mention of the Hermitage. This version of events was going to make a very long walk indeed before breakfast, even if they left very early, as they possibly did.

Alex Murdoch's source of information was Alexander Robertson, Dundonnachie, mastermind of the Dunkeld Bridge toll protest, who would well know how unlikely it was that the friends climbed both Birnam Hill and Craigiebarns before breakfast. It is more than likely that Alexander Robertson had his story of Burn's visit from Peter Murray, the Inver dyer and weaver, who played bass for Niel after his brother Donald's death about 1786. His last appearance is in the rental of 1784 and Niel's lament for his brother appeared in 1788.

At this point, the poet's notes are a little more expansive, a reason to be grateful, for he has left us a happy description of Niel, 'Neil [sic] Gow plays; a short, stout-built Highland figure, with his greyish eyes shed on his honest social brow—an interesting face, marking strong sense, kind open-heartedness, mixed with un-mistrusting simplicity—visit his house—Margaret Gow'. [13]

It is usually assumed that Niel joined them at Dr Stewart's in Dunkeld and that the whole party then made the ferry crossing to Inver to the Gow cottage, there to meet Mrs Gow and resume their music making. They were joined by Peter Murray who names the tunes that were played: 'Loch Erroch side' to which Burns later wrote the lyric 'Oh stay sweet warbling woodlark, stay!' The poet then requested 'Niel Gow's Lament for Abercairney' followed by the splendid 'McIntosh's Lament' and 'Tullochgorm'. Dr Stewart's contributed the march 'We'll take the Highway'. Peter Murray told Charlie McIntosh that Jamie Dewar, the whip the cat (tailor) working at the Gow household that day passed on the information that Burns borrowed a clean shirt from Niel! [14]

The tradition that they all then sojourned to the inn, where Burns scratched a far from complimentary verse on the window pane, is a most unlikely story. There was a window pane in one of the upper windows of the centre building of the inn on which was scratched the names of various visitors. This may have been the source of the confusion. [15]

Following the young poet's visit to Niel at Inver, he now re-crossed the river and set off on the

Niel Gow's Lamentation for Abercairney. [Atholl Collection, A K Bell]

twenty mile journey to Blair Atholl, armed with a letter of introduction to the Duke of Atholl. He was invited by the Duchess to stay at the castle, where he spent two days. Burns's diary of the second day concludes, 'Dance—Sup—Duke; Mr Graham of Fintry; Mr McLaggan; next Mrs Stewart'. Sixty years later on, old Peter Murray informed Dr Robert Chambers that Niel and he played for the dancing that night, giving Burns another opportunity to enjoy their music making. [16]

Records of other visitors survive. In 1801 a young man, William McPherson, set off from Blairgowrie with his tutor, Mr Halliday. Like Robert Burns, they made an early start, arriving at Gourdy some miles away in time for breakfast with friends. They then proceeded on horseback to the Hermitage where they found the gates locked and had to find a guide (possibly Peter Murray) to let them in. Writing to his mother in London, McPherson continues the story:

> ... when we came back again, the gate was locked and the man gone, so that we were obliged to climb over it. In our way there, we passed through the village where Niel Gow lives, he was sitting at the door of his house upon a log of wood, we stopped and talked with him for some time, he said a great many curious things of himself. [17]

How one wishes he had written down these curious things! Another delightful description of a child's memory of Niel is left us by Elizabeth Grant of Rothiemurchus, in 1804:

> On this journey I first remember old Neil [sic] Gow being sent for to play to us at the inn at Inver—not Dunkeld, that little village we passed through and went on to a ferry at Inver, which we crossed the following morning in a large boat. It was a beautiful ferry, the stream full and deep and dark.... I don't know whether this did not make more impression on me than Neil Gow's delightful violin, that it had so over excited me ...that my father had to take me a little walk by the riverside in the moonlight before I was rational enough to be left to sleep. [18]

Her brother William took it all more coolly 'remarking on nothing but the peat reek ...' [19]

A more mature record of Niel's appearance and playing is given us by Dr Garnet, on a tour of Scotland in 1798. He was accompanied by Mr Watts, an artist who made a sketch of Niel which, although done in haste, was considered a good likeness by the doctor. A descendant of Niel, Mrs Mettan, sent me a photograph of her ancestor which had been in the family and to my surprise it was identical to that of Mr Watts' drawing.

The two travellers put up at an inn in Dunkeld where they were favoured with a visit from Niel Gow:

W.H. Watt made this quick sketch when he and Dr Garnet met Niel Gow in Dunkeld. [HJ]

> ... a singular and well known character, and a celebrated performer on the violin. When I call him a celebrated performer, I do not mean that he can execute the sweet Italian.... His only music is that of his native country, which he has acquired chiefly by ear ...; But he plays the Scotch airs with a spirit and enthusiasm peculiar to himself. He is now in his seventy-second year.... He favoured us with several pieces of Scotch music; he excells most in the strathspeys, which are jigs played with a peculiar spirit and life; but he executes the laments or funeral music with a great deal of pathos. [20]

So Niel's skill and enthusiasm for playing was undiminished in his old age. He could still captivate young and old alike.

Later in the evening, the doctor and his companion were invited to join the dancing-school ball being held at the inn. They were impressed by the superior quality of the Highland dancing, observing that the children 'would have cut no disgraceful figure on the stage'. [21] Niel, and indeed the Gow family, were closely connected with the Highland dancing of the period. Dancing has until recently been one of the main recreations of the inhabitants of the whole area, each district enjoying the services of their own 'dancie'. [22]

Niel's daughter Margaret married James MacDonald, a dancing master in Edinburgh, while both Nathaniel and John's offspring married into the family of George Jenkins, dancing master in London, more of which in a later chapter. As late as 1806, by which time Niel was failing, his help was being sought to supply dancers for the Highland Society in Edinburgh. Sir John Sinclair, writing to Mr Palliser, requested:

> There are two persons in Dunkeld who dance Highland dances, emblematic of war and courtship. The convener of the Highland Society wish to have these dances exhibited to

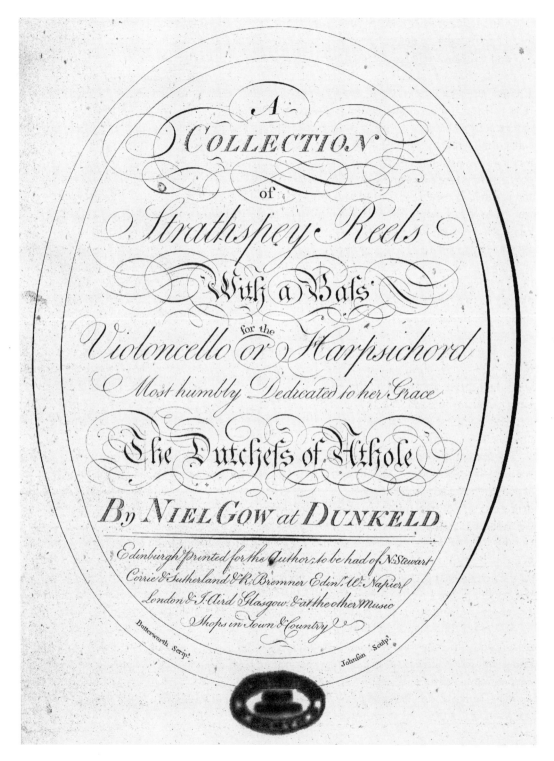

Frontispiece from collection dedicated to the Duchess of Atholl, 1784. [Atholl Collection, A K Bell]

the Edinburgh Theatre on Tuesday next and wishes that men should be sent, so as to be in Edinburgh Monday night or early Tuesday morning. Neil [sic] Gow knows who they are and the tunes that ought to be played, the names of which they should bring with them.[23]

The two men were Alexander Gow and Peter Robertson. 'The Battle' was played by Donald Dewar. 'The Forester's Son' was the ancient sword dance, quite different from the Gillecallum. The last named was, of course, the well known sword dance, the music for which appeared in Niel's first collection of music, published by his son Nathaniel. Much information concerning these dances was no doubt lost with Niel's passing. His boyhood was spent before the imposition of vindictive proscriptions on all things Highland. Pipe music would accompany the old Highland dances, Gaelic songs would be sung and the old harp tunes would still be in circulation. All these the young Niel would absorb as naturally as the Strathbraan air he breathed, to carry with him for the rest of his life. Gaelic stories, too, would still be told round the peat fire, Gaelic customs practised, Gaelic superstitions observed, before the church succeeded in stamping them out. Later in the nineteenth century over-zealous missionaries completed the work in Strathbraan, persuading people to sing their hymns instead of the old ballads. Happily Niel grew up before that cultural devastation, playing on his fiddle the ancient tunes he carried in his head. Fortunately, he passed on many of these fine old melodies, his son Nathaniel preserving them for us in print, as well as Niel's own compositions, those of other members of the family and many of other gifted Perthshire musicians.

Between 1784 and 1806 four volumes of music were published under Niel's name, although Nathaniel was responsible for the editing, canvassing the subscribers and generally overseeing the whole enterprise. Many of the tunes, such as 'Tullochgorm' or 'Gilliecallum' had been in circulation longer than anyone could tell, but others such as 'Niel Gow's lament for Abercairney' and 'Niel Gow's Lament for his second wife' are surely among the most beautiful and poignant melodies ever produced by a Scottish composer.

In order to finance the printing of these volumes it was necessary to ensure support for the venture. This was done initially by dedicating the publication to a number of the aristocracy, in the expectation that the noble houses would be generous in their patronage. The first volume was dedicated to 'Her Grace the Duchess of Atholl', with some subsequent ones to 'The Noblemen and Gentlemen of the Caledonian Hunt', 'The Most Noble, the Marchioness of Tweedale' and 'The Right Honourable, the Earl of Eglinton' showing the wide range of patronage enjoyed by Niel. Another way of ensuring sales was to draw up a list of subscribers willing to purchase at least one volume. These lists make interesting reading in their range of patrons, from nobility to merchants, fellow musicians and neighbours in Inver. Lastly tunes could be titled to honour a lady or gentleman of high rank, or a friend, or a name of a house or a well loved place. These titles also make interesting reading.

We do not know how much of the original character of these tunes has been lost in their transference to notation, given that Nathaniel's editing would be done with a background of knowledge and with sensitivity. Surely we should be grateful that both ballads and fiddle tunes have survived at all.

Niel was fortunate that he had four gifted sons and grandsons to carry on the Gow musical tradition. Sadly, two of them pre-deceased him, William in 1791 and Andrew in 1794.

William, the eldest of the Gow family, was born presumably at Inver in 1751. He would have had a reasonable education at Little Dunkeld parish school, possibly going to Edinburgh to complete his musical education, for he was musically talented. There he became organist for the New English

Chapel in the Cowgate as well as holding the position of leader of the Edinburgh Assembly Band, following the retiral of Alexander McGlashan who may have been his teacher. He also composed a few tunes, the best known being 'Mrs Dundas of Arniston', 'Mrs Muir Mackenzie's Reel' and 'Lady Louden's Strathspey'. William married Jean Lawsen in Edinburgh in 1776, by whom he had three children, Nisbet, Niel and William. When he died in 1791, he left a trail of debts for his hapless children to inherit; a sad and untimely end to an able musician.

Three years after William's death, Niel had the sorrow of losing another son, Andrew, also a talented musician. He was born around 1755 and left Inver to receive a classical training, possibly in Edinburgh. In the early 1780s he went to London with his brother John. They settled at 60 King Street, Golden Square. The brothers were quickly integrated into the musical life of the capital, both serving on the committee of the New Musical Fund which promoted concerts. Andrew was among those who played at the famous performance of Handel's music in Westminster Abbey, commemorating the centenary of the composer's death. Apart from performing, Andrew and John set up a music selling business in Golden Square, from which they also published volumes of dances, the first three of which appeared under their joint names.

Sadly, Andrew's health deteriorated, causing his father grave concern. Niel wrote to John urging him to send his brother home by sea to Edinburgh or Dundee. 'We will have milk which he can get warm from the cow, or fresh butter or whey or chickens. He shall not want for anything.'[24] Despite all the care and attention lavished on him, Andrew died in July 1794.

The final grief suffered by Niel was in 1805 when Margaret, his companion and soul mate for thirty years, died. Theirs had been a unique union of two mature people which, although it proved childless, nevertheless gave to Niel's motherless bairns a secure home. Nathaniel's tribute to his step-mother bears this out, while Niel's elegy to her shows the depth of his emotion.

Thought by many to be Niel Gow's most haunting melody,
the lament for his second wife, Margaret Urchart. [Atholl Collection, A K Bell]

Although no longer able to venture far from home, Niel continued to compose until the last. In 1802 he wrote to Nathaniel, 'Three tunes and three of my own if they are of any use ye are very wellcome to them'. [25] His last composition was 'Dunkeld Bridge' which must have been as late as 1805 for Thomas Telford did not start building until the spring of that year.

Niel's only surviving daughter, Margaret, with her daughter Jemima came from Edinburgh to look after her father in his last days. She was the widow of James McDonald, a dancing master and composer.

In December of 1806 Niel, feeling that death was not far off, sent for the Little Dunkeld minister, Alexander Irvine, that he might set his affairs in order. Ever mindful of the most needy of his family, he left a legacy to Nisbet and William, the orphaned children of his eldest son William. The rest of his not inconsiderable estate of over £1,000, including all his moveable estate, he left to Margaret. [26]

Niel died on the 1 March 1807 and was interred in Little Dunkeld churchyard where his two surviving sons, John and Nathaniel, erected a handsome stone to his memory. The memorial inscription records the names of his two wives, Margaret Wiseman and Margaret Urquhart. [27]

It was the end of an era. The opening of the Dunkeld Bridge in 1809 was to change the character of the village completely. The weaving trade was soon to go into decline, forestry work and saw milling taking its place. The Inver folk could soon cross the bridge to Dunkeld to purchase their clothes in the shops opening in the new Dunkeld street.

In the field of entertainment, young people's tastes were changing, although their elders clung to the old way. The strathspeys gave way to the Schottische, polkas, quadrilles were soon to be the rage and the waltz, at first thought to be rather naughty because the gentleman took the lady round the waist, eventually received the seal of respectability when the young Queen Victoria danced it. Niel would have had difficulty fitting into the new assemblies in Edinburgh and London, although

Niel Gow's gravestone in Little Dunkeld. Damaged and in need of repair, in 1986 it was taken to Dunkeld Cathedral, where it can now be seen in the Chapter House. A new stone was erected in the Little Dunkeld graveyard in 1987. [HJ]

his sons John and Nathaniel had no problem adjusting to the latest fashions.

The young Elizabeth Grant of Rothiemurchus was well aware of these changes as she was happily dancing the new quadrille. But she did feel a pang of sadness, taking a backward glance at the memory of Niel playing to them at the inn. Let her have the last word, 'The next time we travelled the road, the new bridge over the Tay at Dunkeld was finished, the new inn, The Duke's Arms, opened, the ferry and the quiet inn at Inver done up, and Niel Gow dead'. [28]

1. Atholl Archives (hereafter referred to as A.A.) Rentals 1754 7/418
2. Ibid., Accounts 5/141
3. Ibid., 54/2/148
4. Ibid., Bundle 1587
5. Maxtone Graham, *The Beautiful Mrs Graham* (London 1927) 184
6. Ibid., 199.
7. Maxtone Graham, *The Oliphants of Gask* (London 1910) 316.
8. Ibid. 315
9. O.S.A., *Little Dunkeld* p. 411
10. N.L.S. Ms. 590 1600
11. Ed. R.L. Brown *Robert Burn's Tour of the Highlands and Stirlingshire 1787* (Edinburgh 1973) 97
12. Alexander Murdoch *The Fiddle in Scotland* (London 1888) 45.
13. Ed. R.L. Brown *Robert Burn's Tour of the Highlands and Stirlingshire 1787* (Edinburgh 1973) 272
14. Ed. Sir Alexander Muir Mackenzie of Delvine *Tacketies and tyres in Strathbraan* (Perth 1908) 13
15. Remembered by the late Mr Bill Edwards.
16. *Chamber's Edinburgh Journal* 1844
17. Newton Castle Archive, Blairgowrie. 1st. September 1801 William McPherson to Mrs McPherson, No. 1 Queens Place, Hammersmith.
18. Elizabeth Grant of Rothiemurchus *Memoirs of a Highland Lady I* (Edinburgh 1988) 44
19. Ibid., 44.
20. Dr Garnet *Observations on a Tour through the Highlands and part of the Western Isles of Scotland* (London 1800) 73.
21. Ibid., 74
22. *Perthshire Courier* numerous references in the nineteenth century.
23. A.A. 48/7/127
24. Joseph McGregor *Memorial of Niel Gow in a Collection of Reels and Strathspeys* (Edinburgh 1837) 3.
25. NLS MS 590 Nos. 1600–1
26. SRO CCF/7/116/68
27. There is no known description of his funeral but an item in the Parish Poor Fund records that Margaret paid two shillings for the use of the mortcloth and donated one pound to the Fund in memory of her father.
28. Elizabeth Grant of Rothiemurchus *Memoirs of a Highland Lady II* (Edinburgh 1988) 25

Descendants of John Gow and Catharine McEwan of Strath Braan, Perthshire

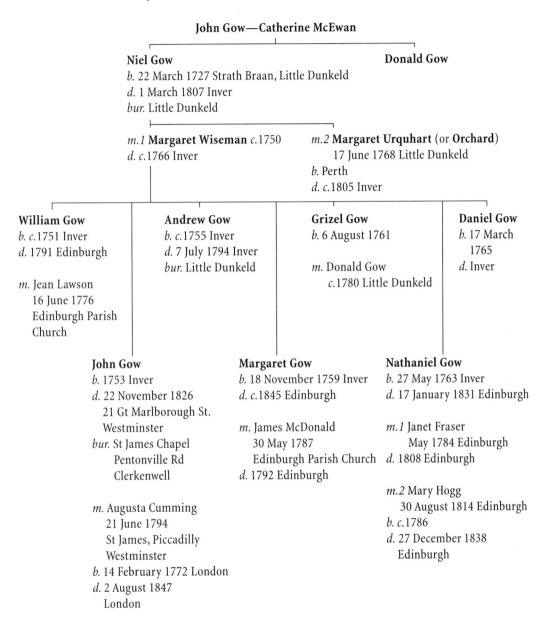

John Gow—Catherine McEwan

Niel Gow
b. 22 March 1727 Strath Braan, Little Dunkeld
d. 1 March 1807 Inver
bur. Little Dunkeld

Donald Gow

m.1 **Margaret Wiseman** *c.*1750
*d. c.*1766 Inver

m.2 **Margaret Urquhart** (or **Orchard**)
17 June 1768 Little Dunkeld
b. Perth
*d. c.*1805 Inver

William Gow
*b. c.*1751 Inver
d. 1791 Edinburgh

m. Jean Lawson
16 June 1776
Edinburgh Parish
Church

Andrew Gow
*b. c.*1755 Inver
d. 7 July 1794 Inver
bur. Little Dunkeld

Grizel Gow
b. 6 August 1761

m. Donald Gow
*c.*1780 Little Dunkeld

Daniel Gow
b. 17 March
1765
d. Inver

John Gow
b. 1753 Inver
d. 22 November 1826
21 Gt Marlborough St.
Westminster
bur. St James Chapel
Pentonville Rd
Clerkenwell

m. Augusta Cumming
21 June 1794
St James, Piccadilly
Westminster
b. 14 February 1772 London
d. 2 August 1847
London

Margaret Gow
b. 18 November 1759 Inver
*d. c.*1845 Edinburgh

m. James McDonald
30 May 1787
Edinburgh Parish Church
d. 1792 Edinburgh

Nathaniel Gow
b. 27 May 1763 Inver
d. 17 January 1831 Edinburgh

m.1 Janet Fraser
May 1784 Edinburgh
d. 1808 Edinburgh

m.2 Mary Hogg
30 August 1814 Edinburgh
*b. c.*1786
d. 27 December 1838
Edinburgh

The Gow family tree can be viewed in full on Perth & Kinross Library's web site, www.pkc.gov.uk

Niel's playing

Contemplating Niel's portrait by Raeburn, it seems as if the violin was an extension of the man himself. They are as one. One observes that he holds the instrument on his shoulder, as was the habit of country fiddlers in those days, not under the chin as classically trained musicians do. The fiddle is supported by his arm, not by his chin. This restricted the players ability to move his left hand from one position to another on the fingerboard. However, as most of the reels and strathspeys that were played were confined to the range of the first position, this was not a drawback.

Turning from the left hand supporting the violin, the eye wanders to the strong right hand holding the bow. It was his individual style of bowing that marked Niel from other fiddlers. The blind judge who awarded the youthful Gow the prize in the competition of skill declared that he could distinguish the stroke of Niel's bow among a hundred players, the other contenders heartily agreeing with him. Professor Baird writes of Niel's playing:

> There is perhaps no species whatever of music executed on the violin which the characteristic expression depend more on the power of the bow, particularly in what is called the upward or returning stroke than the Highland reel. Here accordingly was Gow's forte. His bowhand, as a suitable instrument of his genius, was uncommonly powerful, and when the note produced by the up-bow was often feeble and undistinct in other hands, it was struck, in his playing, with a strength and certainty which never failed to surprise and delight the skilful hearer. [1]

Alas, there were no recording studios in those days and so we can only imagine the magic of his performance. Fortunately, his sons inherited their father's skill and Nathaniel in his teaching must have passed on some of the style to his pupils. Niel himself taught in Inver, where the sound of his violin must have been as familiar to his neighbours as the clanking of the weavers' looms. Surely at least some of this rubbed off, to be passed on by the MacIntosh's, the Hardies, the Crerars and the host of fiddlers who entertained around Inver, Dunkeld, the Bishopric and Strathbraan, where the playing of his music persists to the present day.

1. *Scots Magazine* March 1809 obituary.

Portraits

So much that has been written about Niel Gow is myth with no foundation what so ever that it can be classified as rubbish. Old Mrs McIntosh who was for many years his neighbour, on hearing some of the stories, remarked to her grandson Charlie, 'What are thae awfu' stories they're puttin' on the decent man'. [1] Here we will confine ourselves to the facts. First of all, descriptions of Niel's appearance left to us by people who knew him.

Colonel David Stewart of Garth, referring to the difference in characteristics between the Saxons and the Celts, writes:

> One of the most remarkable of the latter was the celebrated Niel Gow, whose genius has added fresh spirit to the cheerful exhilerating music of Caledonia, and who, although he was born and during the period of a long life, lived, within a mile of the Lowland border, exhibited a perfect specimen of the genuine Highlander in person, garb, principles and character. [2]

Professor Baird, his first biographer, described him thus:

> Though he had raised himself to independent and affluent circumstances in his old age, he continued free from any appearance of vanity or ostentation. He retained to the last the same plain and unassuming simplicity in his carriage, his dress and manners, which he had observed in his early and more obscure days. His figure was vigorous and manly, and the expression of his countainance spirited and intelligent. His whole appearance indeed exhibited so characteristic a model of what national partiality conceives a Scottish highlander to be, that his portrait has been repeatedly copied. [3]

Robert Burns's description of Niel has already been referred to and confirms the previous two word portraits. We have, thus, a clear mental picture of Niel's appearance and demeanour. Let us now examine the portraits.

By far the most famous and the one most frequently reproduced is that painted by Sir Henry Raeburn which is now displayed at the Scottish National Portrait Gallery, Queen Street, Edinburgh. With reference to the painting, Nathaniel, writing to Sainsbury in 1824, states that four admirable likenesses of his father had been painted a few years earlier for the Duke of Athole, Lord Gray, the Hon. William Maule M.P. and the County Hall, Perth. [4] Unfortunately, Nathaniel does not mention when his father sat for Sir Henry, leading to a number of differing opinions about it.

Recent exhaustive research by Dr David Mackie puts the date at around 1790, when Niel was in his sixties. We must remember, however, that by all accounts Niel retained his vigour well into old age. According to Dr Mackie, there are many versions of this work including those mentioned by Nathaniel. In addition, a Mrs Mackenzie is said to have had in her possession a copy made by Raeburn and presented to Niel. If that is so, it is curious that no mention of this portrait is made by Nathaniel. Furthermore, its whereabouts is unknown. Yet another portrait is in the possession of

Niel Gow by Sir Henry Raeburn. [From the collection at Blair Castle, Perthshire]

the Roseberry family, showing Niel supporting a walking stick rather than his fiddle and holding his hat. Dr Mackie also lists a version said to have been owned by Robert Napier, the engineer. [5]

This account will show just how absurd is the oft repeated anecdote concerning the Duke of Atholl arm in arm with Niel, proceeding along Princes Street en route for a sitting with Raeburn.

A version hangs in the fitting setting of the ballroom of Blair Castle, the castle where Niel played on so many occasions and where his music still sometimes echoes through the walls. The copy commissioned by the Perth County Hall can now be seen in Perth Museum and Art Gallery in George Street, Perth

Another interesting likeness of Niel and his brother Donald appears in the painting 'Highland wedding at Blair Atholl' by the Scottish painter, David Allan. [6] Allan visited Blair Castle in the 1780s, from whence he went around the Perthshire countryside sketching, leaving us an accurate record of the houses and the people going about their daily activities. The Gow brothers posed for Allan, who used their figures in other paintings. The 'Highland Wedding' depicts the dancers enjoying themselves out of a summers evening, as was their custom. On the left of the picture is a piper quaffing a dram, no doubt prior to joining in the music making. It is a painting full of interest, especially so as it is the only representation we have of Donald Gow, playing the 'cello.

1. Sir Alexander Muir Mackenzie of Delvine, ed. *Tacketies and tyres in Strathbraan* (Perth 1908) 13
2. David Stewart of Garth, Maj. Gen. *Sketches of the Highlander in Scotland I.* (Inverness 1855) 108
3. *Scots Magazine* January 1809
4. G.U.L. 83, Nathaniel Gow to Sainsbury 1824
5. From an unpublished Ph.D. thesis of David Mackie. Copyright 1999
6. Painting on long loan out at Duff House, Banff, by the National Gallery of Scotland.

Violins

Niel's violins are one of the main subjects giving rise to a rich crop of anecdotes, all equally unbelievable. That he must have had more than one instrument in his long, crowded playing career, goes without saying. There were many fine violin makers in Scotland in the eighteenth century and possibly he played on one of these, say by Matthew Hardie of Edinburgh.

Both Niel's sons, John in London and Nathaniel in Edinburgh, sold musical instruments of all kinds and were well positioned to procure the best for their father. Apart from that, Niel had the means to afford the best, rendering the stories about him wheedling a violin or a bow from a shopkeeper by playing one of his pieces by sight, quite absurd.

There are three instruments in the Perthshire area which purport to be Gow violins, the best known being at Blair Castle. Lord James, 9th. Duke of Atholl, had it examined by William Hill in London who stated that it was an eighteenth century violin with a value of about £200. Jane Anderson, the archivist at Blair Castle, points out to musicians her doubts about the fiddle's authenticity, but people want to believe it is genuine and fiddlers get a thrill playing Niel's music under his portrait in the ball room—a piece of romanticism, in which most of us readily indulge from time to time.

The fiddle, which is said to have belonged to Niel Gow, in the Ballroom, Blair Castle. [From the collection at Blair Castle, Perthshire]

When I read an excerpt from the *Perthshire Advertiser* of 1932 relating the story of a Niel Gow fiddle that had recently been donated to the Perthshire Musical (Competition) Festival by Mr Herbert Pullar, to be competed for in the Scots fiddle class, I was sceptical. Recent information concerning the instrument, kindly released to me by the Festival committee, confirmed my doubts.

The story goes as follows: Samson Duncan (1767–1827) a friend of Niel's, bought the fiddle from him as Gow was hard up. Duncan's son Thomas, an accomplished painter, wanted his father to sit for his portrait. Samson would only consent if his son depicted him holding the fiddle. The fine portrait is in the Perth Museum and Art Gallery. That is the only incontrovertible fact in the story. On Samson's death the violin passed to Miss Duncan, Dunkeld Road, Perth, who sold it to Ignez Wrozina, Edinburgh, along with the above story, saying that Samson had often related it to her. In 1889 Mr Wrozina sold it to Mrs Pullar, Rosebank, Perth, along with a signed declaration as to its authenticity. In due course it passed to her son Mr Herbert Pullar who, in 1932, donated it to the Perthshire Music Festival for competition.

The story was further embroidered. The reason Niel was hard up was that his son Nathaniel was in financial difficulties. Nathaniel's music selling business did indeed have money problems but not until several years after his father's death. It was further averred that Samson Duncan played the fiddle as a member of Nathaniel Gow's band which entertained King George IV on his visit to Edinburgh in 1822. Where these embellishments to the story come from is not known, but they were related to Mr Adam Rennie of the *Perthshire Advertiser* in 1932 and used in a radio programme about Niel Gow, in which Mr Rennie took part, in 1949.

Eventually, in 1986 the Festival committee decided to have the violin examined and valued for insurance purposes. They were advised to send it to Mr Peter A. Lyle M.A., F.T.C.L.,

Thomas Duncan's portrait of his father, Samson Duncan. [Perth Museum & Art Gallery]

L.R.A.M., A.R.C.M., of Ayr for examination. He enlisted the opinion of a violin professor, a player and repairer and a violin maker. Their findings were as follows:

> To the best of our knowledge, the violin appears to date from mid nineteenth century, and is probably of Tyrolean or possible even French origin, despite the Cremona label … with regard to the playing qualities of the violin, it is a fine instrument, responsive and even in tone, and certainly worth playing. As regards the value, we would suggest, in the absence of any more expert assessment, that it should be insured for around £1,500. [1]

The Festival committee, unwilling to pay the insurance on what they no longer believed to be a Niel Gow violin, sold the instrument in 1987. Its present whereabouts is unknown, but it is to be hoped that there is no spurious story attached to it.

I have gone into considerable detail regarding this story to show how wary one has to be in believing the authenticity of any Niel Gow artifacts, unless there is cast-iron proof of its origin.

The last of the three violins mentioned is held by Perth Museum and Art Gallery and bears a silver plate with the inscription 'One of four Niel Gow violins. Presented to Duncan McKerchar Inver Dunkeld by J.R. Findlater C.E. 1851.' This fiddle was presented to the Gaelic Society of Perth in September 1931 under the bequest of the late Baillie Niel Gow. In March 1936 the Gaelic Society decided to offer it on loan to Perth Museum where it has been ever since.

Baillie Niel Gow claimed to be a direct descendant of Niel Gow, Inver, but there is no substance to that claim. His family came from Blair Atholl and, to date, no connection between the Blair Atholl

Gows and the Inver Gows has been uncovered. In an article in the *Perthshire Courier* of 1 November 1927, Baillie Gow stated:

> Niel Gow's fiddle, which was played on before George IV, was presented to me by Major Herbert Pullar of Dunbarney. The fiddle, before being purchased by Major Pullar's mother, was in the possession of representatives of the late Samson Duncan, the famous Perth violinist, who played in Niel Gow's band, and a picture of him with his fiddle hangs on the walls of the Perth Library. [2]

So the Festival violin and the museum violin are both said to have belonged at one time to Samson Duncan and both purchased by Mrs Pullar. There is a confusion here.

What of the label on the museum fiddle? Duncan McKerchar, a well known Dunkeld fiddler, did not occupy Niel Gow's house in Inver until around 1867. [3] The 1871 census finds him still there but he died in Colinton Poorhouse in December 1873. For further information on Duncan Mckerchar, see the following chapter on Perthshire fiddlers. The only Findlater known to have a connection with the Dunkeld area is John Findlater, one time sub-factor to the Duke of Atholl. He is also mentioned as having given an interesting old music manuscript to Charles McIntosh, who later presented it to Lady Dorothea, eldest daughter of the 7th. Duke of Atholl. It is now in the Atholl Collection in the A.K. Bell Library in Perth. [4] So far, the Perth Museum have not had the violin examined by an expert opinion as to the date of the instrument, so its authenticity is still speculative.

Finally there is the story concerning a Caspar de Saló violin, two completely different versions of which have been penned by William C. Honeyman. The first appears in the *People's Friend* on 8 September 1890. [5] He tells the story of Niel and his son visiting Hill's in London, seeking to purchase a violin there. Gow is attracted to the Gasparo but says it is beyond his means. He is, however, allowed to play on it and he so enchants the owner who, in a burst of generosity, gifts the instrument to Niel. Subsequently, in 1880 a Perthshire gentleman takes the same violin to Moritz Hamining in Dresden to be valued. He declares it to be a Gasper [sic] di Salo in Brescia. Inside he discovered a label with the legend 'Broken on the ice at Stairdam in 1784 and mended in Aberdeen.—Niel Gow.'

The second version appears in *Strathspey Players, past and present* by William C. Honeyman, first published postumously [6] in 1922 so when it was actually written is uncertain. On this occasion, Niel acquires the violin from Col. McQuarrie, George Square, Edinburgh, while entertaining at a party. Niel exchanged it for his own. The second part of the story concerns Niel returning from a ball at Dunkeld House, when he fell on the ice at the Stairdam and broke it! [7]

Maxton Graham states:

> Niel Gow was the most celebrated of all Highland fiddlers. The Duke of Atholl retained his services for a fee of £5 to play at all festivities at Blair and Dunkeld House. It was in leaving one of these in the winter of 1784 that he fell on the ice at Stairdam and broke his fiddle. The instrument was repaired and acquired by Mr James Maxton Graham of Cultoquhey in 1871. [8]

No word of its being at Gaspara. The present whereabouts is not know to the writer or to the Maxton Graham family.

I have qualms about repeating these absurd stories and, having shown how unbelievable they are, can only hope that they will be laid to rest. William Honeyman wrote so much of value concerning violin makers and the art of playing Scottish fiddle music, that he is best remembered for that, not for his yarns.

1. Miss Duncan's guarantee stated it was 'made in Tyrol if not in Cremona'.
2. This picture is the one painted by Thomas Duncan which is now in Perth Museum and Art Gallery.
3. A.A. Census 1867.
4. Atholl Collection N27 24682.
5. Although the article is unsigned, Honeyman at that time was employed writing .for the *People's Friend*.
6. Honeyman died April 15th. 1919. The booklet was first published by Largo Son, Dundee and reprinted in 1984 by Fiddletree Music, Richmond Virginia.
7. Niel returning from Dunkeld House had only to cross the Tay in the ferry to reach home. Stairdam is miles off his route, being at the head of Birnam Pass on the old A9 route between Bankfoot and Dunkeld. The Perth to Dunkeld turnpike road was not built until 1793. The old road did not pass the Stairdam.
8. Maxtone Graham, *The Beautiful Mrs Graham* (London 1927) 182.

Memorabilia

There are a few items said to have belonged to Niel Gow but, as with the violins, most can not be authenticated. The lack of anything of value in the inventory of his household goods suggests that Niel disposed of special pieces of furniture before he died. This is in keeping with his character. Margaret, his daughter, was left all that remained. Her daughter had every prospect of being married so no doubt many keepsakes found their way to Edinburgh.

There are only two items that are at present known to be authentic. The first, a glass goblet engraved with the initials N.G., is in the possession of the Atholl family and is displayed at Blair Castle. How or when it came into their possession is not known but it is on record that when Queen Victoria and Prince Albert were entertained by the Athole family at Dunkeld in 1842, Her Majesty was served Athole brose out of Niel Gow's glass.

In the National Museum of Scotland, six items are on show which are said to have belonged to Niel Gow. The only genuine one is a punch ladle with a silver plate inscribed 'Niel Gow's punch spoon presented by his daughter Mrs McDonald to her son-in-law David Foggo 1810'. David Foggo, an English teacher, married Jemima about this time, so it would be possible that this was a wedding gift from Margaret to David.

The remaining five items on display are all 'said to have belonged to Niel Gow'. They are:
1. Fiddle case of wood covered with hide.
2. Printed book *Complete report of original Scots slow strathspey and dances* signed by Nathaniel Gow.
3. Horn spoon which may have belonged to Niel Gow.
4. Wooden ladle with hook for hanging which may have belonged to Niel Gow.
5. Walking stick with ivory disc engraved 'N.G.' said to have been used by Niel Gow.

In connection with No. 5 above, it is interesting to note in the inventory of his household goods are listed '2 walking sticks but supposed not to belong to him'. Perhaps they were left behind inadvertently by visitors. Anyway, one cannot imagine Niel striding out with a walking stick. A cromach would be more likely, if he used anything at all on his travels.

There is a chair on display at Balnain House, Inverness, apparently labelled 'Niel Gow's chair'. It is said to be on loan from the Saltire Society but so far it has been impossible to find out any further information concerning it.

The Gow family is spread far and wide. William, John and Nathaniel all had family, many of whom married. Augusta, Nathaniel's daughter, had twelve children, some of whom contributed richly to the musical life of Tasmania, where she emigrated with her husband Frederick Packer in 1852. In a letter to the Duchess of Atholl in 1872 Augusta told Her Grace that she possessed the family Bible, inscribed. Miss L.A. Cannon, London has been in contact with Hobart Museum in Tasmania to see if any museum there holds the Bible, but so far without results. Now what a find that would be!

John and Andrew Gow

Of all Niel's offspring, his second son John was by far the most prosperous. With his younger brother Andrew, he settled in London around 1780 at 60 King Street, Golden Acre. By that time both, along with their eldest brother William, all had received a classical music education, where is not known but most likely in Edinburgh.

The Highland Society of London was formed in 1778, its aim being to further the cause of Highland culture in language, music, poetry and dance. In 1784 they engaged John Gow to play at their meetings for a fee of £10 10s. per annum, his duties to commence in November of that year. By January 1785 John had incurred the displeasure of the committee when he announced that he would be unable to attend the Society's meeting as he was engaged to play at the opera house. However, there must have been a happy resolution to the difficulty for John continued to entertain the Society with his playing, for in 1822 they presented him with a gold medal 'In testimony of their appreciation of his long service and of the delight which his eminent and hereditary musical talents have never failed to inspire at the meetings of the Society.' The medal is decorated with the armorial bearings of the Duke of Atholl, inscribed 'Clann nan Gadheal ann guallibh á chiele' translating as 'Children of the Gael, shoulder to shoulder'.

While he was busily engaged with Highland music for the Society and playing at the opera, he was preparing tunes for publication. In 1788 *12 Favourite Country Dances and 4 Cotilions for the Violin, Harpsichord or Harp-Book 1st.* appeared, published by W. Campbell, London. Over the next thirty years or so, John produced ten more collections and arrangements of Scottish reels, strathspeys and quadrilles as well as containing items from opera. The first two volumes were produced in collaboration with his brother Andrew, the second of which was dedicated to the Highland Society of London. It contained ninety tunes. Some of these volumes were published in London, some in Edinburgh. The first three volumes were for violin with a bass for 'cello, harpsichord or piano, but being an astute business man with an eye for a growing demand, his later arrangements were for the piano. Nathaniel both arranged and published the volume appearing in 1819, while the last two were in collaboration with his son John Horne Gow, who by that time had joined the business.

Both John and Andrew were actively involved in the New Musical Fund, London, which promoted concerts from time to time. During Joseph Haydn's second visit to the capital in 1794–95, he was invited to conduct his symphonies at a concert organised by the Fund. A feature of musical life in London at that time were the commemorative performances of Handel's Messiah in Westminster Abbey, the first of these taking place in 1784, followed by others, the last being in 1791. John and Andrew both took part in these occasions but whether as violin or viola players is not known. The two brothers played both these instruments.

1794 was an eventful year for John Gow, bringing him both sorrow and joy. His brother Andrew's health declined. Urged by his father to return home to Inver, he sadly died there later that year. A happier occasion took place in June when John married Augusta Cumming in St James's Westminster.. She was the daughter of Alexander Cumming, a prestigious watchmaker and chronologist who had come from Edinburgh to set up business in New Bond Street, London.

John and Augusta set up house in Great Marlborough Street where they brought up their children, Niel born in 1795, John Horne born about 1797, Elizabeth who sadly died aged two years and Augusta. In 1803 John moved his business to 31 Carnaby Street, then in 1815 to Great Marlborough Street and finally, in partnership with his son John Horne, to 162 Regent Street.

John died a wealthy man in November 1826 and was buried in the crypt of St James's, Pentonville Road, Clerkenwell. The crypt was cemented over in the 1960s to make way for a community centre and the unidentified remains, including John's, were re-interred in communal graves at the East London Cemetery. Fortunately, the stones had been recorded in 1884 by F.T. Carswick. It records that 'The various duties of husband, father and friend he faithfully and affectionately discharged. His integrity was strict and unblemished, his probity to man exemplary, his confidence in God sincere.'[1] A true son of Niel.

1.   F T Carswick, *Inscriptions of the remaining stones of St James's Pentonville Road* 1884

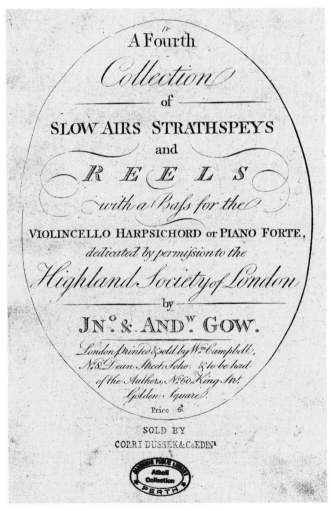

The frontispiece John and Andrew Gow's fourth collection, 1793. [Atholl Collection, A K Bell]

Nathaniel Gow

Nathaniel, the youngest surviving son of Niel and Margaret Gow—Daniel, the youngest seems to have died in infancy—most faithfully carried on the tradition of his father. Born in 1763, educated under Mr Foggo in Little Dunkeld Parish School, while still in his teens Nathaniel was packed off to Edinburgh by his father to finish his musical education, first under Robert McIntosh and Andrew McGlashan who taught him violin and later his 'cello teacher was Joseph Reneage, with whom he kept up a lasting friendship. At some point, too, he also studied trumpet, for he was appointed King's Trumpeter at the age of nineteen. This duty entailed accompanying the Justiciary judges on their circuit tours, playing fanfares at royal proclamations and, gruesomely, attending executions. This post he held for life.

Dancing was a popular recreation in Edinburgh when young Gow arrived there. From the formal Assemblies of the upper echelons of society to the more unrestrained parties of the so called ordinary folk, reels and strathspeys were the delight of all. Supplying music for them gave employment to musicians. Nathaniel grasped the opportunity and was soon playing at the Assemblies, first under Mr McGlashan, then under his brother William and then, on his death in 1791, taking over the leadership of the music himself.

By this time, Nathaniel had realised that there was a likely market for publishing volumes of dance music, [1] his first collection appearing in 1784 when he was only twenty years of age. The list of subscriptions is interesting. Of the subscribers, seventy three were from titled families, including twenty two Perthshire landowners. The legal profession was well represented, comprising forty writers to the signet and seventeen advocates. There were also ten dancing masters and twenty eight musicians from London where surely John and Andrew had been busy and even seven excise officers. Starting off with such a wide range of support, the success of the volume was assured. The subscribers' list also illustrates the popularity of Scottish dances in all classes of society at that time, although the price of five shillings put it beyond the reach of working men who, in any case, would have been unlikely to have the ability to read the music or possess the instrument to play it on.

The success of the first volume was followed by three others in 1788, 1792 and 1800. By the time the second collection appeared, John and Andrew had established themselves as music sellers in London and were able to promote sales there. Although all the titles to these collections were under Niel Gow at Dunkeld, they in fact included tunes by other composers, but Nathaniel himself arranged the tunes and supplied the basses.

Nathaniel's twenty first year was also memorable for his marriage to Janet Fraser on 17 August 1784. Margaret, their first child, was born in 1785, four other daughters in the following years and, finally, the much longed for son in 1794, named Niel after his grandfather.

In 1796 Nathaniel started a new venture when he set up business as a music seller and publisher at 41 North Bridge Street. There he worked in close co-operation with his brother John who ran a similar establishment in London. They dealt widely in musical instruments, both new and second hand. By this time the harpsichord was giving way to the piano in popularity. Both brothers exploited this new market, arranging their dance music for piano as well as harpsichord and stocking instruments made by John Broadwood, a Scotsman who carried on a business near John Gow in Golden Square, London. Nathaniel also employed a piano tuner who undertook piano repairs. Violins made by Edinburgh violin makers were sold and all manner of wind instruments were retailed and repaired. In all this, he worked closely with his brothers as the following letter, dated 1797, shows:

> Last order went yesterday for Leith on board the Commercial Packet Joseph Morely. The Drum you ordered went along with them it is not painted yet but any coach painter can do it.... The price of it is £4.4.0 and a case to put it in 5 shillings.... If you send us whiskey ... Augusta [his wife] says she does not mean to be confined when she drinks it....[2]

It was never Nathaniel's intention to engage himself in the day to day running of the business. That was left, unwisely as it turned out, to William Shepherd. Shepherd was no businessman. When he died in January 1812 the accounts were in a state of confusion, no cash or day book ever having been kept, nor any record of the stock held. An accountant had been called in to examine the books which showed many customers and suppliers owing money. The company, which had temporarily been run by young John Shepherd, was dissolved in 1813, Nathaniel paying off every penny of the debts.

By this time Nathaniel was a wealthy man, being even more generously patronised by the noble families than his father. No fashionable gathering was complete if Gow was not leading the dancers. He was paid £100 to 150 guineas to appear at Perth, Dumfries or Inverness. On his frequent visits to London he was invited to play with King George IV who was a 'cellist, as well as playing at royal parties.[3] He also had a flourishing teaching connection at his home in Princes Street, as well as travelling once a week to Dalkeith Palace to teach the children of the Duke of Buccleuch.

In the midst of all this activity he continued to publish volumes of music, mostly supplied by his father of Niel's own composition, as well as those of others. Nathaniel himself composed such popular dance tunes as 'Largo's Fairy Dance' but his best known work is 'Caller Herrin',' written with the cry of the Newhaven fishwives along George Street against a background of the church bells of St George's Church. First published in 1810 as a piece for the piano, Baroness Nairne later added words to it. Since then many composers have made instrumental and vocal arrangements of this popular tune. These works were first published by Gow and Shepherd, but later in partnership with Niel Gow junior.

1805 was a sad year for Nathaniel when the death occurred not only of his step mother, but also his wife, leaving him with a family of six, the three youngest ranging in age from fifteen to nine. Margaret, the eldest, however was now twenty and able to look after them until she married in 1810. Her husband was Adam Armstrong, of farming stock from Dalkeith, who had recently purchased Drum colliery with £8,000 lent him by his father-in-law. But shortly after their marriage, foreign imports caused the colliery to fail, Nathaniel losing all his money. Adam and Margaret went to England, then to Wales. Margaret died some time after the birth of their sixth child Christopher. Thereafter, Adam decided to emigrate to Western Australia with his young brood, where he flourished working with land he acquired. His delightful descendants are proud of their Scottish ancestry and their illustrious forebears. Things did not turn out so well for Nathaniel.

In 1810 he was involved in a breach of promise lawsuit, brought by Mary Hog. It does not seem to have soured their relationship for they were married two years later and Augusta, their daughter, was born in 1815. A talented musician, Augusta studied music at the Royal Academy of Music where she met Charles Pacuer, also a musician, from Reading. They emigrated to Hobart, Tasmania, where Charles and his sons laid the foundations of the musical life there. John, their second child, was born in 1821. One of his descendants lives in Elgin where she has called her band appropriately 'Gow Now'.

Nathaniel's son Niel, a clever lad, became a doctor after studying in London and Paris. He returned to Edinburgh in 1818 where he and his father set up in business at 60 Princes Street. About this time James Hogg, the Ettrick poet, visited Edinburgh where he met young Niel. They collaborated in writing two Jacobite songs 'Flora MacDonald's Lament' and 'Bonny Prince Charlie'. Niel also composed dance music including 'The Marchioness of Huntly's Favourite' and 'Miss Hay of Hayton's Reel'.

This was a prosperous time for the Gow family, which was increasing, Mary bearing three sons and two daughters. Nathaniel was busy during the daytime producing volume after volume of dance music containing many tunes of his own composition as well as those of his family and other composers. He also taught violin, commanding the highest fees for his services, while his evenings were taken up playing at house parties and balls organised by the Caledonian Hunt. He was in great demand further afield in Perth, Dumfries, Inverness and London. Perthshire fiddlers were not

'Caller Herring'—one of Nathaniel Gow's best loved tunes. [Atholl Collection, A K Bell]

forgotten, with such as James McIntosh and Samson Duncan being invited to join his band. The highlight of his playing career was undoubtedly the visit of King George IV to Edinburgh in 1822. The Duke of Buccleugh arranged a banquet for His Majesty at Dalkeith Palace, engaging Nathaniel and his band to play. King George, recognising Gow from his visits to London, advanced to greet him, expressing his pleasure at meeting him.

It was a year later that Nathaniel's successful lifestyle started to crumble. The first blow fell with his son Niel's death in 1823. A clever, gifted young man, he seems to have kept control of the music business as well as taking an active part in the musical life of the city. A year later, Nathaniel's career came to an abrupt end when he was seized with a paralytic stroke. He tried to keep the business going by acquiring as a partner a piano tuner from Broadwood's in London by the name of Galbraith. It never really worked, finally closing down in 1829 when his bankruptcy was advertised in June of that year. The music stock was sold off, as was the property in Hanover Street where he had carried on his teaching. Of his two surviving children, Augusta was just twelve and John six. For them, the outlook was bleak.

His patron of old, the Earl of Dalhousie, rallied support by organising a ball which was then held annually to raise funds, while Nathaniel petitioned King George IV to be put on the Exchequer's Roll to receive a pension. Thus the family managed to survive until Nathaniel died in January 1831.

With his death, the Gow family's contribution to Scottish music came to an end, for though various members of the next generation showed musical ability, none reached the heights, nor had the charisma, of old Niel and Nathaniel. We will never know what their playing sounded like, but Nathaniel has left us a record of the music that they performed, although the printed page cannot tell us the manner in which it was done. Their industry never ceases to amaze. Their exuberance, which so inspired the dancers, has become the stuff of legend. The life style of Niel's family in Edinburgh and London was far removed from their parents' simple rural existence in Inver, but their Perthshire roots were never forgotten as the titles of many of their airs show. Niel and his family have left us a rich legacy which we would do well to nurture, keeping it bright for future generations to enjoy.

1. Several volumes had already appeared in Edinburgh by 1780 e.g. Adam Craig *A Collection of Choicest Scots Tunes* 1730, Daniel Dow *A Collection of Ancient Scots Music* 1778 and Neil Stewart *A Collection of the Newest and Best Reels and Country Dances* 1761.
2. NLS 590/1707
3. NLS Dep. 341 No. 69 Nathaniel's biography

John Crerar

Niel passed on his characteristic style of playing through his teaching, firstly through his sons whom he taught on a kit violin, this is a small violin which dancing masters in the eighteenth and nineteenth centuries carried around with them in their pockets, its size making it possible for them to play the music while demonstrating the steps. It was a useful instrument which was also, because of its size, suitable for teaching children. Nathaniel was the only son whom we know for certain taught violin, thus passing on to another generation his father's style of playing. There is little doubt that many budding Scottish fiddlers listened to Niel's playing and tried to emulate his bowing technique, but we have no way of knowing how successful they were.

Apart from his own family, including Margaret who may well also have had lessons from her father, the only pupils of Niel outwith his family of whom we are certain are John Crerar and James McIntosh.

John Crerar was born in 1750 at Ferniehaugh, Dunkeld, the second son of Alexander Crerar, fowler to the 2nd. Duke of Atholl. David Allan portrays Alexander in a painting of the 4th. Duke and Duchess with their family. When he was sixteen years of age, John received lessons from Niel paid for by the Duke. [1] He entered the service of the 4th. Duke of Atholl in 1776, according to Lady Dorothea, [2] as a keeper and stalker, continuing in that employment for the next fifty years. During that time he set about organising stalking in the deer forests, which until then had received little attention. He was described by Scrope, the author of *The Art of Deer Stalking*:

> The king of sportsmen and good fellows. . . . He was honest, faithful and most attached adherant , of astonishing active powers. . . . He was also a composer of music, and many a dance have the lads and lasses had to the sound of my old friend's fiddle. [3]

When the Duke was away from home, Crerar regularly sent him letters, commenting on the vagaries of the weather, what the country folk were getting up to et cetera:

> The House of Filar has been Broak and Eighteen Bottles of wine drunk . . . the smugglers were the rogs. [4]
> Beginning of last week there came three Boats full of Whisky, sum where below the joining of Tumble and the Gary. At the Boat of Port na Craige one of the Boats hett upon a rock, oversett, one man lost, one got out By one of the oars, the third By a hold of one of the Barrels of Whisky. [5]
> The country people goes through the Forest picking up fawns . . . the people have been making it there business to carrie the fawns home, and every young chap in the country has a cap of there skins. [6]

As well as entertaining those around him with his fiddle, Crerar also composed several dance tunes, although it is not always possible to confirm which were his and which may have been circulating around Atholl for years before, for example 'The Merry Lad of Inver' and 'The Big Boat of Inver'.

43

These two tunes are reproduced in *Tacketies and Tyres in Strathbraan* with the observation that the first was a local reel but might have been by John Crerar. The author states that the second tune used to be lilted about Inver, that he had from an old manuscript book and that it was likely to be the work of a local composer. [7]

Four of Crerar's earliest tunes are published in Alexander McGlashan's second edition of a *Collection of Reels: consisting chiefly of Strathspeys, Atholl Reels with a bass for the Violin 'Cello or Harpsichord* 1786. [8] They are 'Forest Lodge', 'The Duke of Atholl's Forest', 'The banks of the Garry' and 'The Bridge of Garry at Struan'. Lady Dorothea, writing of this collection, is of the opinion that Crerar probably also wrote other local reels in this collection, such as 'The Marquis of Tulliebardine'. Another Crerar tune, 'Craigie Barns', was published in Gow's *Second Repository*.

The other dance tunes in the manuscript are unpublished, all with titles having a local connection and bearing his signature. The scripts are rough and ready, but easily decipherable. Which of us would care to write music with a quill pen? The names are 'Lady Emily Percy's Welcome to Scotland' (1810), 'Lord James Murray's Wedding Day' (1810), 'General Glenlyon's March and Quickstep', 'The Honourable George Murray's Strathspey', 'Miss Charlotte Murray's Reel', 'Miss Frances Murray's Reel', 'The Bridge of Dunkeld', 'Miss Mackenzie of Delvine's Jig', 'Quick Step for the young knight (Delvine)', 'Lady John Scott of Binchat', 'Lord John Scott's Strathspey' and finally 'The Beinn a Ghlo Hunt' which Lady Dorothea notes 'is still played at Blair on the pipes'.

Landseer's painting, 'The Death of a Stag in Glen Tilt', which hangs in the Ballroom of Blair Castle, portrays John Crerar along with his son Charles. They are part of a group depicting the elderly 4th. Duke John with his grandson Glenlyon. The Duke had a great regard for John Crerar,

Payment to Niel Gow for teaching John Crerar, 1766. [AA 5/139]

'Lady John Scott of Binchat' by John Crerar, thought to be written in his own hand.
In 1836 Lord John Scott rented 8,000 acres of Atholl deer forest,
where John Crerar worked as a forester. [Atholl Collection, A K Bell]

who had kept him abreast with news of the estate over a period of some sixty years. Writing in his diary in 1824, the Duke notes, 'McIntyre ill, Crerar old, Charles Crerar too young and myself disabled'.[9] When he died in 1830, the Duke left John an annuity of £25, which despite his eighty years, he was able to enjoy for ten years.

John Crerar died 1 March 1840 and he lies in the family burial ground of Dowally churchyard. The inscription on the tombstone, erected by Marjory, Duchess of Atholl, bears the tribute, 'Esteemed and respected by all who knew him, he was for upward of half a century constant and faithful attendant of John Fourth Duke of Atholl, in the sports of the forest, the field and the stream'.

1. A.A. Accounts 5/139 Oct. 1766 'To Niel Gow fiddler a years salary £5 and for Teaching young Crerar £1'.
2. A.A. Bundle 1466. Most of this account of Crerar is taken from Lady Dorothea's item.
3. Ibid., 1466.
4. J Stewart Murray *Chronicles of the Atholl and Tulliebardine families IV* (Edinburgh 1908) 314
5. Ibid., 314
6. Ibid., 358
7. Ed. Sir Alexander Muir Mackenzie of Delvine *Tackets and Tyres in Strathbraan* (Perth 1908) 6 & 10. The old manuscript is possibly the one in the A.K. Bell Library, given to Lady Dorothea by Charlie McIntosh.
8. Atholl Collection 011 24728.
9. J Stewart Murray *Chronicles of the Atholl and Tulliebardine families IV* (Edinburgh 1908) 359

Merry lads Macintosh

Three generations of the Macintosh family made music in Inver and the surrounding area for upward of one hundred and fifty years. Although no doubt influenced and helped by both Niel and Nathaniel Gow, their music making was of a different order from that of the Gows, most noticeably in their enthusiasm for singing.

Charlie Macintosh, the founder of the family, arrived in Inver in the early 1780s having come down from the north disguised as a woman in order to escape the clutches of a press gang which were recruiting young men for service in the East India Company. He set up home as a weaver in a two roomed, stone built, thatched cottage across the road from Niel Gow. His grandson, Charlie, described the interior of this house thus, 'Going first into the kitchen we find that the floor consists of mother-earth, beaten hard with the tread of many feet yet not so hard as to be cold or uncomfortable as stone would be . . . "ben the hoose" was carefully floored, with deal flooring'. [1]

The kitchen fireplace was wide and open, over which hung a swey with a hook and chain suspending a large iron pot. Fuel consisted of wood from the nearby plantations or peat brought down from Birnam Hill. A cruisie provided light. It consisted of two iron cups with spouts, placed one inside the other, the upper cup holding whale oil from which a cotton wick projected over the spout so that drops of oil fell into the cup below. Under the cruisie, a book shelf held the family reading matter, Bibles both in English and Gaelic, along with a dictionary of the Bible and concordance, theological and devotional books and for 'lighter' reading *The Man of Feeling* by Henry Mackenzie. Sleeping quarters consisted of box beds in both rooms.

Here Charles Macintosh brought his bride Jean Forbes in 1788; here he reared his family of four sons and two daughters and here he wove his linen on two looms, with a warping mill in the loft. On Sunday the loom was silent while Charles adopted his role as precentor, [2] in which church is unclear. Coates [3] states that it was Dunkeld Cathedral and that once a month, along with the minister of Little Dunkeld church, the Rev. Dr Alexander Irvine, he walked to Lagganallachy beyond Rumbling Bridge in Strathbraan. These services would be in Gaelic.

We have no record of the first Charles Macintosh as a fiddler although he saw to it that his children were all taught violin. Charles, the third son, had the greatest talent although

James Macintosh 1791–1879. [HJ]

brothers James and Donald were both a fiddlers. The latter was the manager of the manufacturing firm Baxter Bros. & Co. Dundee, but kept up his connection with Dunkeld, walking there by Coupar Angus to play all night at a ball led by his brother Charles' band. Their sister May also played the violin, an unusual thing in Inver in those days as it was mostly the lads who were the fiddlers.

Charles senior died in 1833, leaving his wife Jean to be cared for by their daughter Elizabeth [4] until she reached the grand old age of ninety.

James, the second son of Charles the founding father, was born in 1791. As a young lad he was sent across the road to have fiddle lessons from his venerable neighbour, becoming Niel Gow's last pupil.

James served his apprenticeship as a joiner, following his trade in Dunkeld. When working on the restoration of the choir of Dunkeld Cathedral, he lost his snuff mill. Workmen, carrying out further restoration work a century later, recovered the mill, which can be seen in the Chapter House Museum of the Cathedral.

At the invitation of Niel's son Nathaniel, he was part of the band which entertained King

Charles Macintosh 1797–1867.
Detail from the portrait by MacNab,
Perth Museum and Art Gallery. [HJ]

George IV on his visit to Edinburgh in 1822. James decided to pursue his musical career in the capital, becoming a member of the famous Julian Band. Originally called the Reel Players, there were sometimes as many as twenty performers in this select group of the leading Scottish musicians. Based in Edinburgh and conducted by Mr Julian, the Julian Band travelled throughout Scotland and as far afield as the north of England, playing Scottish reels at assemblies and balls. James also established himself as a teacher of violin as well as composing a few reels and strathspeys.

Although he settled in Edinburgh, James never forgot his Perthshire roots, regularly returning to Dunkeld to stay with his nephew, also named James, and play in his band. When an old man of eighty six he made his last visit there to play at the opening of the City Hall in Dunkeld in 1876. The Dowager Duchess Anne was present, accompanied by her grandson the six year old Marquis of Tulliebardine. Later she said to the child 'What a pity you did not shake hands with old James Macintosh, for he was taught the violin when a boy by Niel Gow, and Niel Gow played before Prince Charlie, when the Prince was entertained by a former Marquis of Tulliebardine, so that would have been a link with the '45'. [5]

James Macintosh died in Edinburgh three years later in 1879 and, according to Alexander Murdoch, lies buried in Dalry cemetery there. [6]

Old Charles' third son, also Charles, of all the Macintosh sons, followed most closely in his fathers footsteps. He was born in 1797, receiving a good schooling at Little Dunkeld Parish school under the hard working domini McAra. Unfortunately, where he received his musical training is not known. He was ten when old Niel died, although he averred to his son Charles that he'd never heard Gow play. This is hard to believe. An intelligent musical boy must have absorbed some of the master fiddler's style. Anyway, with his two elder brothers playing, there was obviously music going on around him. Perhaps Peter Hardie, who was in Dunkeld at that time and who played in Niel's band, taught him. Whoever it was, the young Charles had a good grounding in musical theory as well as violin playing. He was also a good singer, inheriting this from his father.

When he left school Charles helped his father with the weaving trade which at that time was still flourishing for the Macintoshes at Inver, though hardship had overtaken some of their neighbouring weavers. In 1833 his father died and three years later he married Mary Cameron from Murthly. The young couple set up home in another stone built 'but and ben' up the brae nearby, but Charles continued to use the looms in the old house where his mother and sister still lived. In the cottage on the brae, the young couple brought up their family of three sons and a daughter. As the children grew bigger the Duke, noticing that their cottage was too cramped, had an extra storey added, with skylights in the slated roof. Son Charles leaves us a description of the house:

> Instead of the open hearth of Grannie's cottage, we find an iron grate, in which some coal is burning, as well as wood from the mill. The cruisies have disappeared and in their place are home made candles, produced either by repeatedly dipping the wick into melted fat, thus forming what are called 'dips'; or else by use of metal candle moulds, into which the fat was poured, generally two moulds at one time. [7]

Mrs Macintosh, Mary Cameron, 1805–1896. Detail from portrait based on a J.F. Mackenzie photograph, Perth Museum and Art Gallery. [HJ]

This description is followed by a comparison of their diet with that of former days. Although essentially oatmeal based, white bread was also available, as was butcher meat, while tea was the most favoured drink. At the end of summer the home-fed pig was killed, the pork salted and hung from the rafters to be used by the family throughout the winter.

Reading matter was also more varied. Perthshire newspapers were read, and no doubt discussed with neighbours, and their mother's interest in natural science catered for, the children's school books and of course the father's collection of music. Included in the furniture was a harmonium which was used at family worship on a Sunday evening—although no such instrument was permitted in church.

By the 1850s hand loom weaving had declined, linen giving way to cotton, forcing the Inver weavers to seek alternative employment. It was then that Charles Macintosh embarked on a successful musical career.

By the time the Free Church had been established in Little Dunkeld following the Disruption of 1843, Charles acted as precentor and choir trainer there. His services as a violinist were in great demand at balls and country houses as well as social gatherings in the villages around. Like Niel before him, he tramped on foot to Blair Atholl and Lude, while nearer to home there was Dalguise House and Murthly Castle, although after 1856 he would be able to get there by train. He was delighted when, in 1863, the railway was extended to Inverness, enabling him to get to more distant venues by train.

At the end of August 1844 Dr Robert Chambers was invited to spend two days at Logierait inn as part of a shooting party. It was his first experience of a grouse shoot or net fishing and it made such an impression on him that he wrote a detailed description of his stay. [8] During the two evenings they were entertained by Charles Macintosh who, on this occasion, was accompanied on the bass by Peter Murray, by now an octogenarian. All were in high spirits as they watched a display of dancing by the villagers who performed with 'frantic gesticulations and intertwinings—such wildly joyous exclamations' on a raft-like boat on the River Tay. Later, in the parlour of the inn, Charles gave them a selection of reels, interspersed with slow airs of Niel and Nathaniel Gow, Donald Dow and Marshall.

On the second day the party crossed the Tay by ferry, heading for another day in the hills above Balnaguard, this time to go fishing on Loch Skiach. On this occasion they were accompanied by Charlie, who cheered them on their way with his fiddle. After a morning's fishing enlivened by bagpipe tunes from a piper, a picnic lunch was enjoyed after which Charlie sang. As they were looking across the Tay to Atholl his appropriate choice was 'Cam ye by Atholl' followed by 'The Braes of Balquhidder'. [9] An elderly follower who had been handling the nets then gave the smugglers song written by the Dunkeld poet Alexander Stewart, which at that time had not yet appeared in print. It relates to a true incident at Corrymuchloch Inn in the Sma' Glen when smugglers routed a party of Scots Greys, sent to confiscate their whisky.

The highlight of Charlie's playing career must have been when he was part of the band that entertained Queen Victoria and Prince Albert on a truly splendid occasion when they visited the Earl of Breadalbane at Taymouth Castle in 1842.

Apart from his playing, he was also much in demand taking singing classes for both children and adults throughout Perthshire. The plan was to go for one month to some small community, take classes and at the end of the month present a concert by the pupils, which was quite an achievement. March 1861 saw him in Strathbraan at the tiny community of Wester Balachraggan, which nevertheless could muster fifty scholars for the final concert. The *Perthshire Advertiser* reported the occasion, 'At the appointed hour the school assembled . . . and the singing showed that the labours of their talented teacher had not been in vain. Very great praise is due to Mr McIntosh considering that few of those under his charge knew anything of music'. [10]

Unfortunately the items performed were not reported but the repertoire must have been limited. After the concert, dancing commenced to the strains of the fiddlers Mr Macintosh and Mr Macfarlane from nearby Aldville. 'Strangers were wholly excluded from the ball and the scholars really enjoyed themselves as their smiling faces amply testified. The greatest good feeling and decorum was preserved during the whole evening.' [11]

At the end of it all, Charles would walk the four miles or so back home. Not a bad evening's work for a man of sixty four years.

He also composed music, some of which has been copied by Lady Dorothea Ruggles-Brise, the eldest daughter of the 7th. Duke of Atholl. The manuscripts can be examined at Blair Castle Charter room. They are of uneven quality but two of the more attractive tunes are a strathspey and a reel dedicated to Miss Murray Threipland of Fingask in the Carse of Gowrie. Probably they were composed for the occasion when Charles was invited to play there by Sir Patrick Murray Threipland in December 1841. The letter of invitation runs thus:

> Sir
> My ladies and myself are anxious to hear your playing again, and as there are one or two young people to be with us on Friday 31st. inst., I wish you would come down and give us a spring that day. Your best way would be to come down by the Dunkeld coach to Perth on Thursday morning, and you would get out by a coach which leaves Perth at a quarter before one o'clock. Of course I shall pay all your expenses going and returning. [12]

In *A Perthshire Naturalist* these two tunes dedicated to Miss Murray Threipland are reproduced as the work of son Charlie, but as the musical examples in the book were supplied by Mr Alexander Sim, who by that time was in Aberdeen, it is a very understandable error. Lady Dorothea clearly marks them along with others as the work of Charles Macintosh senior.

This hard working, dedicated musician died on November 4 1867, leaving behind two sons, James and Charles, to carry on the tradition of music-making in Inver.

The third Charles Macintosh who has already flitted through these pages from time to time, was born at Inver on 27 March 1839. Best known as a naturalist, he also made an interesting contribution to the musical life in the area. By the time he was school age (children in Scotland started school around six years of age,) he could already read having been taught by his mother, who was a highly intelligent woman.

A great schism in the Church of Scotland known as the Disruption took place in 1843, when a large number of clergymen along with many of their congregation, broke away from the parish church to form the Free Church of Scotland. The Macintosh family was one such household in Little Dunkeld to do so. The newly formed church had neither churches to worship in nor schools in which to educate their young. To meet this latter need a wooden building was erected at the foot of the Birnam Glen, near where the Beatrix Potter garden now is. There was, of course, no village of Birnam at that time, this spot being known as Wester Inshewan. This was the school that young Charlie had to trudge to, where he was taught the three 'R's by the school's first master, John Sutherland.

During the summer months he worked as a herd, employed by local farmers to keep sheep, cattle and goats from straying onto the crops growing in the unfenced fields. Another source of employment for boys was holding horses drawing coaches which pulled up at Inver inn on their way from Breadalbane to Perth. When he was fourteen years of age Charles attended the Royal Grammar School of Dunkeld, where the excellent Mr Lowe was the rector. Under his guidance Charles was introduced to the delights of astronomy. Later, when Mr Lowe retired to Inver, this interest continued, Charles eventually acquiring his own telescope. During his two years at Dunkeld

Charles acquired the rudiments of science, mathematics, Latin which was to prove of use to him later as a naturalist and advanced English.

Meanwhile, at home his father was teaching him to play the violin, along with the elements of music theory. Singing was as natural as breathing in the Macintosh household. His mother was also a dominant influence, passing on her interest in natural history to her son.

When he was sixteen Charles had to seek work. Sawmilling was the main source of employment in the village so it was natural that Charlie should join the work force there. His job as a sawmiller came to an end when his hand was caught in a saw, depriving him of all the fingers and thumb of his left hand. As well as ending his employment, the accident meant that he could no longer play the violin. But Charles did not let his disability debar him from instrumental music making. He found that his injured hand could find its way up and down the frets of a 'cello. He was now able to play in his father's band and, later, his brother James'.

Meantime, in 1858 he started work as a rural postman, walking over to Dunkeld post office to collect the mail which he then delivered to all the little villages and hamlets on the east bank of the Tay, heading north for Tulliemet. After spending the night there, he walked the return journey to Dunkeld. He did this for five years until the Highland railway was extended to Inverness. This occupation gave him the daily opportunity to observe all the wild life of that area and he became an expert naturalist.

Charles Macintosh' cottage. From an original drawing by Colin Gibson. [Mrs Gillian Zealand]

His next beat took him along the Bishopric on the other side of the Tay as far as Kinnaird House. Dalguise House lay along this route and it was when he was delivering letters that he first encountered the young Beatrix Potter, on holiday there. Later, she was to recall:

> I can remember him since July 1870, swinging up the avenue with long strides and head down, and a very small child sent to 'get the letters' waiting under a copper beech. Perhaps I remember this because, on that first occasion I ran away—I don't know which of us was the shyest! He was a keen observer and first rate naturalist . . . the kind of student who would continue to learn throughout a long life. [13]

Charles retired in 1890 at the age of fifty one. After thirty two years of tramping in all weathers, his health could no longer take the strain. In all that time the most he earned was fourteen shillings a week. His pension amounted to ten shillings a week, on which he had to live in his cottage in Inver for the next thirty years. Fortunately his interests were wide, but his life style was simple.

Shortly after his retiral, in the summer of 1892, he had another encounter with Beatrix Potter who, with her parents, spent the season in a villa behind Birnam Station. By this time Beatrix, now approaching thirty, had become very knowledgable about fungi. Aware that Charlie Macintosh was an expert in the many mushrooms in the area, she was anxious to seek his help. Their mutual friend, the photographer A.F. Mackenzie, arranged a meeting. In her journal for Saturday 29 October 1892 she records:

> Accordingly by appointment he came, with his soft hat, a walking stick, a little bundle, and very dirty boots, at five o'clock to the minute. He was quite painfully shy and uncouth at first, as though he was trying to swallow a muffin, and rolling his eyes about. He was certainly pleased with my drawings, and his judgement speaking to their accuracy in minute botanical points gave me infinately more pleasure than that of critics who assume more, and know less than poor Charlie. He is a perfect dragon of erudition, and not gardeners Latin either . . . I asked him to sit down, his head somewhere in the chandelier. I would not make fun of him for worlds but he reminded me so much of a damaged lamp post. He warmed up to his favourite subjct, his comments terse and to the point, and conscientiously accurate. [14]

A correspondence developed between the two mycologists, culminating in a learned paper on the spores of fungi which Beatrix presented to the Linnaean Society. Because she was a woman, she was not allowed to read it herself, its worth rejected by the all male body. Later, her findings were discovered to be entirely accurate. This 'Fascinating acquaintance' between Beatrix and Charlie was celebrated under that title in an exhibition in the Birnam Institute in 1999. Also on show were reproductions of the exquisite paintings of fungi done by Beatrix at this period. The originals are in Perth Museum and Art Gallery, where they lay for many years, the initials H.B.P. unrecognised as those of Beatrix—her full name being Helen Beatrix Potter.

Their correspondence lay wrapped in a brown paper parcel in a press in the house of his niece, Miss Elizabeth Macintosh, Dunkeld, until recovered by Dr Mary Noble, a well known Scottish mycologist who has done much research into the work of McIntosh and Potter in the Dunkeld area. Inver itself, because of its surrounding woods, was a happy hunting ground for Charles, who found many specimens of fungi hitherto unknown in Britain and three, one in Perth, one in Dunkeld and one in Inver, new to science.

But Charles' interest in natural history was not confined to mushrooms. It was noted in the chapter on schools that his knowledge of the local flora and fauna was shared on outings with children, as were the interesting geological features of the area. He also studied meteorology, making daily recordings of rainfall, barometrical pressure and temperature which were then sent to Perth Museum. His recordings of rainfall were also sent to the Rainfall Organisation in London who had recruited him as one of their many nationwide observers . For many centuries, communities situated on the banks of the Tay have been subjected to floods from time to time. These inundations he recorded by cutting notches on the bark of a tree which can still be seen at the point where the Inver lade flows into the Tay. He also recorded droughts by cutting grooves on a rock in the Tay near Inver. In an abnormally dry season, these marks can still be seen.

Finally, Charlie's contribution to the musical life of Inver and the surrounding area was considerable. He followed his father as precentor in the Little Dunkeld Church in 1875, holding that position for twenty five years at the end of which he was presented with a diamond pin and gold watch chain.

He was a keen member of the Birnam Institute, which was founded in 1884, serving on its entertainment committee during its first ten years or so. At this time, too, he formed the Birnam Musical Society, which gave many concerts at the Institute. His connection with the Institute also included a donation of mosses found locally, as well as specimens of mounted ferns. Charles, of course, also played for dances at the Institute as a 'cellist in his brother's band.

His keen interest and knowledge of music in Inver in former times led to another unusual friendship, this time with Lady Dorothea Ruggles-Brise. She was an avid collector of the works of Perthshire musicians, amassing a vast collection of volumes of Gow, MacDonald, Jenkins and Robert McIntosh but she was also keenly interested in early manuscripts, volumes of songs, poems and ballads. Of particular relevance to Inver are the fragments of manuscripts of John Crerar, Peter Hardie and Charlie himself. This invaluable collection, known as the Atholl Collection, she bequeathed to the Sandeman Library, Perth, which is now rehoused and known as the A.K. Bell Library.

In the archives in the Charter Room at Blair Castle are to be found many manuscript copies of music compiled by Lady Dorothea. These include examples of tunes by Charles Macintosh. Lady Dorothea enjoyed talking to Charles on her visits to 'the little house at Inver'. She recalls them thus:

> My friendship with Charles dates from a considerable number of years ago, when I used to stay at Dunkeld House. We had many interests in common. At one time I was anxious to learn all I could of the old Dunkeld fiddlers—and I had collected the published works of the Gows, the MacIntoshes, Malcolm MacDonald and Dow of Kirkmichael, together with the later manuscripts of Crerar, McKerracher and Peter Hardie. These were a source of keen interest to Charlie McIntosh, for some of them he had never seen. I was able to exchange with him the unpublished compositions of Crerar, while he gave me the strange wild melodies of Peter Hardie. [15]

One of Charlie's musical interests was collecting bothy songs and fiddle tunes which circulated in the district, possibly brought through the village by farm workers on their way to Dunkeld or

Charles Macintosh, naturalist and musician. [Mrs Malloch]

James Macintosh 1846–1937. [HJ]

One of Charles Macintosh's bothy ballads. [Atholl Collection, A K Bell]

Perth feeing market. Lady Dorothea recalled, 'He also provided me with fragments of "bothie songs", but they are indeed only fragments, for more often than not he could remember but a few lines. He would sit on the edge of the table and sing or whistle the airs for me, and I would "put them down".'[16]

These fragments, which can be studied in the A.K. Bell Library in Perth and at Blair Castle, are interesting both from the aspect of the words and the musical content. They were far travelled. One ditty, relating the story of the lad from Mingulay travelling to the feeing market in Glasgow, (one of the largest feeing markets for the west of Scotland including the islands) is also quoted in a book on Caithness farming life.[17] This, along with some others, appear in the appendix.

Charlie's own compositions are of less merit than those of either his father or brother. It is disappointing that he drew on the staid Victorian church hymnal rather than the more melodious folk tunes which were floating around Inver at that time. It is interesting that he disliked Lady Dorothea reading the baudy titles of some of the tunes in the old collections. Perhaps he collected these airs, but the words of the ballads were too coarse and rude in character for the douce church choirs and evening classes for which he was writing. The end result is dull. Missionaries were very active in Strathbraan in the nineteenth century, persuading people to forget their Gaelic songs in favour of sacred ones.

Here is a final glimpse of the friendship between the lady of the castle and the humble cottager:

> Once only I offended him. He told me : 'I have an old torn book upstairs; it is no use to anyone; you may have it.' He brought down an old MS book of jigs, dated 1733. 'This is a curiosity' I said. 'I would rather not rob you. Will you let me buy it?' 'In that case,' answered the old man, 'I will put it in the fire' suiting the action to the words. I pulled the little book out of the flames just in time.... [18]

Charles taught the local children violin starting them, as Niel Gow had done with his children, on a small violin. The fact that all the fingers and thumb of his left hand were missing did not seem to affect his teaching, recalled Mrs Malloch, neé Peg Edwards. He also wrote out beginners tunes for her. Tosh, as he was affectionately known to his neighbours in Inver, was also a wood turner so he made Peg a music stand: no need to go to the expense of music books or stand when her handicapped teacher could supply all that was required. 'Charlie's house was a shambles, as he looked after it himself.... Bits of fungi, ferns and various specimens littered the rooms around his microscope.' [19].

This modest, quite remarkable man, died in his brother James' house in Dunkeld on 5 January 1922. He lies buried in Little Dunkeld churchyard near that other great Inver musician, Niel Gow.

James, youngest son of the second Charles Macintosh was born in Inver in 1846. Like his elder brother, he too became a post runner and, like his father, he was leader of a band. The most memorable event of his childhood occurred in 1854 when James was herding cattle near the Hermitage grounds. Hearing a commotion on the nearby road, he ran to see what was the cause and found the Royal Mail lying overturned. He quickly sped to find his mother who, along with other Inver women, rushed to the assistance of the passengers, one of whom chanced to be Count Roehenstart, grandson and last surviving relative of Bonnie Prince Charlie. The women attended to him along with the other travellers and the count rewarded them with a sovereign to purchase ribbons for themselves. Sadly, the count died of his injuries at Dunkeld, where he is buried at the Cathedral, a tombstone marking the grave. The ladies, meantime, had purchased Royal Stuart tartan ribbon in Dunkeld. The Macintosh favour can be seen in the Chapter House Museum there.

James could scarcely fail to be interested in fiddle playing with music making going on all around him. His grandmother too, in her old age, enjoyed telling the lad about her famous, one time neighbour, Niel Gow. When he was a boy, Duncan McKercher was a frequent visitor to the house, joining in the music-making. James began playing fiddle in his father's band along with his brother Charles who, before his accident, played fiddle. He was also part of a group who toured Angus and the Mearns as far as Aberdeen, where he was introduced to Sandy Skinner, brother of Scott Skinner, the beginning of a lasting friendship.

When his father died he started his own band, in which Charles played 'cello. They were engaged each year to play at the gillies ball at Blair Castle. Here is how he remembered these splendid occasions:

> These were days when dances were dances of course. They used to start between eight and nine in the evening and go on until six o'clock in the morning. We used to think we were very early if we went home at 5a.m.... I saw the birth of the eightsome reel, watched its slow rise to popularity.... [20]

He also started a flute band which was much in demand to play at Masonic functions, parades of the Carpenters' Friendly Society and at the opening of the Free Church in Dunkeld by the Earl of Dalhousie in 1874. [21]

At the late age of forty seven, James married Agnes Murray in 1893, when he left Inver to set up house in Dunkeld. There he raised a son, Cameron, and a daughter Elizabeth, who features in the publication *Dunkeld remembered*. [22] He was also a very gifted photographer, going around the district with his camera recording events and worthies of Dunkeld. These have been preserved as glass positives and make interesting viewing when they are shown from time to time in the Birnam Institute. [23]

At the grand old age of eighty six, James Macintosh's collection of *Reels, Strathspeys, Marches etc.* was published by Paterson Sons, music sellers in Perth. Their titles reflect his love of the area 'Inchmagranachan', 'Loch Ordie', 'Inver Woods', and a jig 'Nellie Jackson'. She was the wife of the Inver innkeeper in 1861.

Reflecting on the changes in social dancing which he had experienced throughout his long career, James reminisced, 'I started playing when the vogue for reels and strathspeys was at its height. When some of the old players died out I saw the vogue almost die out with them, but we preserved it and kept it alive for years.' [24]

James attributed the decline in the popularity of the old dances to the increased speed at which the younger generation played them. 'The reels require a somewhat slow rhythmic measure, but they started playing them quickly, and the dancers, in order to keep time, cultivated the vigorous whirl....' [25]

Perhaps this was the reason for the dancers being tired out by two in the morning, much to James' disgust. His final advice to young players was 'Take time and pay heed to the measure and rhythm'.

The Macintosh dynasty in Inver and Dunkeld came to an end with the death of James in 1937. They had carried on Niel's tradition of music making for over a hundred years. More than that, Charles with his great contribution to our knowledge of the natural history of the area, and James with his camera recording the people and events around him, enriched the lives of those around them and left us a legacy which we should cherish. James lies buried in Little Dunkeld churchyard near his brother Charles. Sadly, no gravestone marks the spot.

1. Henry Coates, *A Perthshire Naturalist* (London 1923) 23
2. The person who precented or lead the psalmody at Presbyterian services at a period when organs in church were frowned upon.
3. Henry Coates, *A Perthshire Naturalist* (London 1923) 39
4. Elizabeth's life is referred to in the chapter on women's work.
5. Henry Coates, *A Perthshire Naturalist* (London 1923) 90
6. Alexander Murdoch, *The Fiddler in Scotland* (London 1888) 73.
7. Henry Coates, *A Perthshire Naturalist* (London 1923) 68–69
8. *Chambers Journal* Sat. 19 Oct. 1844 Price 1½d.
9. In Lady Dorothea's manuscript book there is an alternative version of this song, by Charlie Macintosh.
10. *Perthshire Advertiser* 7 March 1861
11. Ibid.
12. Henry Coates, *A Perthshire Naturalist* (London 1923) 85

13. Henry Coates, *A Perthshire Naturalist* (London 1923) 123–124
14. Linder, *The Journal of Beatrix Potter 1881–1897.* (London 1989) 305
15. Henry Coates, *A Perthshire Naturalist* (London 1923) 111–120.
16. Ibid.
17. 'Jenny Horne' *Idylls and sketches of Dalmachair* (Dingwall 1931)
18. Henry Coates, *A Perthshire Naturalist* (London 1923) 120. This was the Dixon manuscript.
19. Recording of Mrs Peg Malloch at Inver 13 August 1988
20. In an interview for the *People's Journal.*
21. This recalls the Fox Maul family's long connection with the musicians in Inver, when Niel used to break his long walks to Aberdeen at Brechin Castle.
22. Published 1993 by the Dunkeld and Birnam Historical Society, Dunkeld.
23. Now in the keeping of Mrs Haxton, Birnam. The Dunkeld Cathedral Museum and Archive have many of them on slides.
24. *People's Journal*
25. Ibid.

Macintosh Family Tree

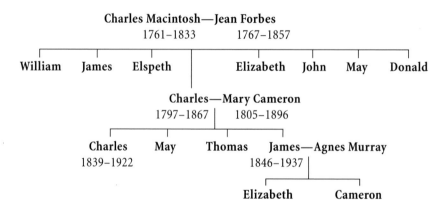

George Jenkins

George Jenkins, a dancing master first and composer second, has no known connection with Inver. The justification for including him in this roll call of Inver musicians is his strong connection with the Gow family.

We meet him first in London in 1788 when he appeared before the committee of the Highland Society to put to them 'A collection of Gallic Airs' which he said he collected from the native music of the songs of the Highlanders. Jenkins wished to dedicate the publication to the Society. Although the secretary promised to mention the collection to the Society at large, there is no evidence that it was ever published. [1] However, a collection of *Eighteen Airs for two Violins or German flutes and a Bass dedicated to Her Grace the Duchess of Atholl* was published by Brysson in Edinburgh in 1789. [2] The one hundred and twelve subscribers to this volume are interesting as they differ widely from those of a later collection since they are all Scottish with the exception of two from London, one from Virginia and one Irishman resident in St Andrews. The rest are mostly from Fife, Dundee and Perthshire.

Five years later his next collection of *New Scotch Music consisting of Slow Airs, Strathspeys etc. dedicated to the Prince of Wales* was published in London in 1794. The subscribers list reads like something from Debrett, with no fewer than five members of the Royal family.

Jenkins next appears in the minutes of the Highland Society in February 1791 when his 'two boys who danced at the company's anniversary meeting . . . the unremitting attention of their father Mr Jenkins (the violin 'cello) to the monthly meetings, have each a Highland dress complete at the expense of the Society' at a cost of £17. 14s. 9d. which also included a piper's Highland dress. [3] Papa was also given a gratuity of ten guineas for his past services as violoncellist, with an allowance of five guineas per annum in time to come. By 1792 however, the Society were growing weary of the boys appearance at their monthly meetings, as their minutes record 'Ordered Mr Jenkins' sons be informed that their attendance will not be required at the next monthly meeting—and that they will be timeously apprised when they are to attend afterwards.' [4] There is no further record of them having entertained the Society.

George Jenkins was appointed dancing master to the Princess Charlotte, daughter of the Prince of Wales, later King George IV, in 1801. The following year he dedicated to the Royal pupil a 'Shantruse' consisting of 'Five favourite airs as danced by Mr Jenkins' scholars, some of which are composed and the whole arranged for the Piano Forte by Nathaniel Gow, by whom thay are also printed and sold'.

By far the best known of George Jenkins compositions is 'The Marquis of Huntly's Highland Fling', the first and only tune to bear the title 'Highland Fling'. It was published in Niel Gow's second repository in 1802, attributed to the late Mr Jenkins. His death appears to have been unexpected for the payment for his services to the Princess was made in March 1803. Thereafter his son James carried on giving dancing lessons to the Princess. The other son apparently gave lessons at Shrewsbury House, Shooter's Hill, her summer residence, from 1801–1804. His address in the accounts is given as 19 Devonshire Street, Portland Place. This was probably the W.K. Jenkins who married Mary Gow, Nathaniel's daughter. James Jenkins married Augusta, John Gow's daughter and

Elizabeth Jenkins married Niel Gow, John's son. This, along with the fact that George Jenkins played 'cello for John at the Highland Society meetings and no doubt on the many occasions when John was engaged to play at Scottish gatherings in London, indicates a very close connection with the Gow family. [5]

1. N.L.S. Minutes of the Highland Society of London.
2. Atholl Collection BC6826738. Lady Dorothea has pencilled in the date and publisher. All the tunes are un-titled except for the last which is 'The Duchess of Atholl's Minuet'.
3. N.L.S., H.S.L. minutes Feb. 1791
4. Ibid., Feb. 1792
5. A scrap of doggerel appears in Lady Dorothea's manuscript book at Blair Castle, bearing the title 'Jenkins's lament for the loss of his friend 1794' referring to Andrew Gow.

Duncan McKercher

Duncan McKercher [1] was born in Kenmore in 1796. His place of birth is often given as Inver, when in fact he lived there for only a short period of time. [2] The census records of 1841 show him living in Dunkeld with his wife Clementine, but more than likely he came there before that. He was employed as a guide to show tourists around the extensive Atholl gardens at Dunkeld House. By that time he was also established as a musician, playing at house parties and public concerts. The Atholl accounts show him being paid for attending balls at Blair Castle, for instance £2. 10s. in 1835 and £1. 5s. in 1839.

Nothing is known of his training as a musician, although he claimed that he was a pupil of Niel Gow. This is doubtful as he was only eleven years of age when Niel died. Niel, in declining health for some time before his death, was unlikely still to be teaching at this time.

McKercher's style of playing is a matter of differing opinions. James Allan of Forfar, who played along with McKercher in Julian's Band, had, according to Dyer, held McKercher's short 'nippety' style of bowing in contempt, [3] which quite contradicts Charles McIntosh's father who always said that McKercher's style of playing was nearer Niel Gow's than any other he had heard. [4] This view coincided with that of Murdoch who heard him play in the Glasgow City Hall Saturday evening concerts, where McKercher frequently appeared. He described the playing as that of a 'fiddler of the genuine Neil [sic] Gow school'. [5]

What is not in doubt is his showmanship, which earned him the soubriquet 'The Atholl Paganinni' from Fox Maule who was tenant of Birnam Lodge for many years. Murdoch gives an excellent description of McKercher's appearance, 'He was a dapper little man, dressed in a long black surtout coat, and on special occasions he appeared on platforms adorned with his masonic apron, and with a picturesque tartan sash across his right shoulder.' [6]

He was wont to play 'The Mason's Apron' wearing his masonic apron and ending by throwing up his arms, fiddle in one hand, bow in the other.

From the mid 1860s until his death, he occupied Niel Gow's old cottage, previously a ruin, but by that time restored. In addition to his popularity on the concert platform, he was also in great demand as a teacher in Perthshire. McKercher published three books of tunes, but like so much in his life, the source of some of

Duncan McKercher 1796–1873. [HJ]

61

these is a matter of doubt, some apparently being the work of Captain Daniel Menzies. The second collection is part of the Atholl Collection in the A.K. Bell Library, Perth. The tunes are arranged for violin, violoncello and pianoforte, and the volume is dedicated to the Right Honourable Lady Elcho.

According to Murdoch, he was taken ill in Edinburgh in November 1873 and his last public performance was at one of Mr James Lumsden's Scotch concerts. He died in Edinburgh Infirmary the following month. [7] It is sometimes stated that he died in poverty in the Colinton Poorhouse. This is hard to believe, when his services were in such demand right up to the end of his life. Mary Alburgher sums him up thus, 'Although McKerracher was styled the "Atholl Paganinni" his showmanship excelled his musicianship (thence perhaps the title?)'. 8 Amen to that!

1. There are various forms of spelling of his name. The one chosen here is as it appears in the 1871 census.
2. 1871 census parish of Little Dunkeld
3. Henry Dryerre Blairgowrie, Stormont and Strathmore Worthies (Blairgowrie 1903)
4. Ed. Sir Alexander Muir Mackenzie of Delvine *Tackets and tyres in Strathbraan* (Perth 1908)
5. A.G. Murdoch *The Fiddler in Scotland* (London 1888) 74–75
6. Ibid. p75
7. Ibid. p75
8. Mary Ann Alburgher *Scottish fiddlers and their music* (London 1983) 119

Peter Hardie

Peter Hardie is another Perthshire fiddler who had a connection with Niel Gow although it is doubtful if he ever had lessons from him. However, Charlie McIntosh claims Hardie played in Niel's band and must therefore have absorbed his style of performance. It is also in various sources stated that Peter Hardie had a connection with the famous Hardie violinists of Methlick, Aberdeenshire. This might well be true, but so far no such link has been uncovered.

According to his death certificate, Peter Hardie was born in Perth in 1777, the son of Richard Hardie, his mother unknown. This is unusual. Whereas the father is sometimes unknown, it is rare for the mother's name to be so. It may have been that the grandson James who reported the death in 1863 simply didn't know. The name Richard, however, was carried by succeeding generations of Hardies. His letters preserved in Blair Atholl archives are those of a man of some education, especially in the matter of precision of information concerning calculations of measurements for walls and fencing. This skill would greatly assist him in the much finer work of violin making.

By the beginning of the 1800s he had arrived in the Dunkeld area, exactly where and in what capacity is not known. He married May Hutton, the daughter of Joseph Hutton, a farmer in Fungarth, about two miles north east of Dunkeld but in the parish of Caputh. It must have been at this time that he played with Niel, by then an old man. In 1810 a son George was born to Peter and Mary at Dunkeld. Nothing more is known of them until 1822. Batters are all that remains of an old family Bible among the Hardie papers in the A.K. Bell Library, revealing that the family was then at Bridge of Don in Aberdeenshire. [1] The Hutton family tree states that Peter Hardie was employed as a gamekeeper to the Marquis of Huntly, possibly the reason for his presence in Bridge of Don.

The family returned to Perthshire in 1825 when Peter was appointed ground officer to the 4th. Duke of Atholl. He was given the extensive Middle District of the Atholl estate which extended from Dunkeld to near Pitlochry. Like John Crerar before him, he was keen to track down poachers. Crerar, by this time an old man, still kept a look out for them and passed on information to Peter. Peter was given a cottage at Balledmund in Tullymet. Although the house was comfortable enough, the ground around it was a wilderness. Peter, with his usual energy and thoroughness, set about enclosing it to make a decent garden for the family. It was all worth while for he was to live out the rest of his life there.

In January 1828 tragedy struck the family at Balledmund with the death of their son. His wife May was dying and Peter himself was ill. Peter remarried in September of that year. His bride, thirty years his junior, was Margaret Cameron from Strowan.

Duke John died suddenly in 1830, leaving the estate in some confusion. The Middle District was split between the late Duke's trustees and Lord Glenlyon, his son. Peter's wages, amounting to £28. 19s. per annum, were the responsibility of both parties. Unfortunately, Lord Glenlyon's factor sometimes forgot to pay him. By 1837 the situation was intolerable and Peter decided to go, intending to earn his living as a musician. [2]

As has already been mentioned, little is known of Peter's younger days or where he received his musical training. The Atholl accounts show him being paid £4 along with John Fleming, also from Tullymet, for playing at balls at Blair Inn and Blair Castle.

Manuscript copies of music in the Atholl Collection show exercises for fiddle indicating that he possibly taught as well as played the violin. There are also dance tunes, but perhaps his best known composition is his lament for Sir Robert Dick who lived in Tulliemet House neighbouring Balledmund Cottage.

Charlie Macintosh also states that Hardie made violins, which again points to a relationship with Matthew Hardie, one of Scotland's foremost violin makers of the eighteenth century, in Edinburgh. According to Charlie, Duke John commissioned him to make violins of larch wood. This is quite possibly true as the Duke was responsible for planting thousands of larch trees on his estate and was always anxious to see to what use larch could be put.

Of Peter's sons little is known, except for John who was a shoemaker in the area. The census records for Dowally for 1851 and 1861 designate Peter a musician, but by then the old couple must have fallen on hard times for his death certificate in 13th. August 1862 records him as a pauper. His son John no doubt predeceased him as his grandson James informed the registrar of his death. Peter lies buried in Dowally churchyard. Sadly, no stone marks the grave, although later members of the family are recorded on a separate stone up to the present century.

I have gone into some detail about Perthshire Peter Hardie as so much confusion has arisen concerning the connection between the Perthshire and the north-east Hardie families. Perhaps some genealogist would take up the tale and find the link.

1. Atholl Collection.
2. A.A. 1095. He was allowed to stay at Balledmund for a rent of £3 per annum.

Peter Hardie's 'Lament for Sir R. Dick' in the hand of the composer.
Major General Sir Robert Dick of Tulliemet was killed in action at Sobraon 1846. The tablet erected by the 42nd Royal Highland Regiment to commemorate his distinguished military career is now in Dunkeld Cathedral. [Atholl Collection, A K Bell]

Malcolm McDonald

Malcolm McDonald is an intriguing character as so little is known about him. It is suggested that he might have died at Inver but the Poor Lists of Little Dunkeld Church, which lists the hiring of the mortcloth for the burial of those who died, does not contain his name. Likewise, his place of birth is unknown, although the predominance of Perth and Perthshire subscribers to his second collection of strathspeys and reels suggests that he was well known throughout the county. Of these subscribers the presence of so many from the Breadalbane area, coupled with the dedication to the Earl of Breadalbane, suggests that he might have come from that district.

Neither was he born at Inver, at least there is no record of his birth in the Old Parish register. What is known, however, is that he lived in Inver, although he does not appear in the rentals, [1] therefore he must either have been in lodgings or living rent free, quite a possibility on the Atholl estate. We are grateful to Charles Macintosh who confirms this by stating that his father told him that McDonald lived in the west part of the village. Many of the old houses in that area were pulled down in the nineteenth century.

Malcolm McDonald produced four collections of strathspeys and reels, spanning the years 1788 to 1797. Of these, the first is dedicated to Mrs Baird of Newbyth, West Lothian the second to the Earl of Breadalbane, the third to Miss Drummond of Perth and the fourth to the Countess of Breadalbane, suggesting an affinity with the Breadalbane district. [2] The names of the tunes in the first collection (1788) also suggest a connection with the north of Perthshire and Breadalbane rather than Atholl. Be that as it may, never the less we are grateful to Malcolm McDonald for leaving so many fine tunes of his own, as well as those of his contemporaries.

1. There was only one McDonald family in Inver in the late eighteenth, early nineteenth century and a Malcolm was most certainly not one of them.
2. The Breadalbane district in north west Perthshire lies roughly from the junction of the rivers Tay and Lyon to the west of Tyndrum, comprising the basin of the upper Tay.

Alexander Sim

Although not an Inver man, mention is made of Alexander Sim because he took the Perthshire tradition of music making to Aberdeen.

Born in Birnam into an old Little Dunkeld family, his father John was an able musician, playing both violin and 'cello. Alexander received his early fiddle instruction from James Macintosh, becoming a member of his band. He too entered the postal service, initially working in Birnam. When he passed his exams as a telegraphist he was posted to Aberdeen where he started the Strathspey and Reel Society. In Aberdeen he had further lessons on the violin, this time in the classical tradition. Like his friend Scott Skinner, and in our own day Alastair Hardie, he believed that a classical training in no way conflicted with the playing of reels and strathspeys, the superior technique acquired enhancing their performance of Scottish music. Niel Gow, who saw to it that all four of his sons had a sound classical training, would surely have agreed with him.

Local musicians
Left to Right: *Jim McLean, Dunkeld; Alexander Sim, Birnam; James Macintosh, Dunkeld; John Scott, Inver; John Lamb, Dunkeld. [HJ]*

John Scott

Like Charlie Macintosh, John Scott was an Inver man, a postman and a talented musician. He played the violin and taught the instrument to many local children as well as running a popular band which entertained at concerts and dances. Practices were held in the Scott's house on Saturday night with Mrs Scott providing delicious home baked refreshments midway. The band's repertoire included Highland reels and the practice always finished with a reel and a strathspey. Peg Malloch, remembering those happy evenings, said she sometimes could not easily settle to sleep when she went home as the music merrily continued in her mind. Bill Edwards recalled that at dances where John Scott's band played in the Birnam Institute and at many small venues in the area such as Balnaguard School, 'There was no hoochin' or carrying on. If you started hoochin', John Scott would cry out "Stop the band!" The band went on just the same, but he didn't like people bawling and shouting their heads off. He was a great fellow—a great chap!'

John Scott's Band 1925.
Back row, left to right: *Sandy Bain; Peg Edwards; M. Smith; S. Fraser.*
Centre row: *J. Lawrie; A. Buchanan, Jnr.; J. Robertson; C. Carr; ? Levison.*
Front row: *A. Buchanan, Snr.; J. Sim; J. Scott; J. Stewart; Mrs Scott; J. Bruce. [Mrs Malloch]*

Duchess Unveils Memorial to Niel Gow

On the wall of the little cottage at Inver, near Dunkeld, which was the birthplace of Niel Gow, a bronze plaque was dedicated on Wednesday to the memory of this renowned fiddler, composer, and collector of traditional music.

The unveiling was performed by Her Grace The Duchess of Atholl, who told the story of Niel Gow's life, and recalled his friendship with members of her husband's family. Although he had to travel to Grandtully for his violin lessons, Gow showed promise at an early age, and when only 18 he entered for and won a contest in which the the rivalry was so keen that a blind judge was appointed to ensure fair play. This official remarked that he would recognise Niel Gow's bow among all the others he had ever heard.

Gow, continued the Duchess, was born in days when instrumental music was frowned upon by the Kirk, but after the '45 rebellion—when the pipes, as well as the kilt and the tartan, were banned - the violin came into its own as a dance instrument. Niel Gow became the greatest player of Scottish dance music, and also performed a great service by writing down and publishing traditional tunes which might otherwise have been lost.

" I think we may take a special pride in these tunes today," con-cluded Her Grace, " because while in Niel's time, this dance music became more and more popular in Scotland, to-day it does not stop at the borders; it has invaded England and seems in the process of capturing London. People who are not Scots, and who have no connection with Scotland are danc-ing reels, strathspeys, and every other kind of country dance with avidity."

The ceremony was presided over by Lord Kinnaird, Lord Lieutenant of Perthshire, who remarked that Niel Gow lived to-day in his music, " I hope that for many generations to come we shall still do honour to Niel Gow in remembering his music," he added.

The plaque was dedicated by the Rev. T. Roger Gillies, Little Dunkeld, and votes of thanks to all who had made the memorial possible were proposed by Mr J. Moodie, musical director of the Carnegie Trust. Mr Moodie re-marked that the fact that the memorial had been erected nearly a century and a half after Gow's death testified to the quality of his music. and the contribution he had made to Scottish life and culture.

Lord Provost J. Ure Primrose, Perth, Provost G. T. M'Glashan, County Convener, and Lord James Stewart Murray, were among those at the ceremony.

The plaque has been erected by the Niel Gow Memorial Fund, whose secretary, Mr Alastair Reid, Dunfermline, was responsible for arranging the ceremony.

Niel Gow's Legacy

While Niel Gow's melodies are today known and appreciated in all corners of the world, in Highland Perthshire the magic of his music has come down directly via many talented local musicians. The Dunkeld Reel and Strathspey Society regularly entertain in the area and they always feature some of the well loved Gow tunes. One of the healthiest signs of the long term, musical vitality of the Inver-Dunkeld area is the number of children attending the Royal School of Dunkeld who are learning a variety of instruments, including the violin. It can be no accident that this part of Perthshire is also home to an amazing concentration of musical talent including Hamish Moore, piper and pipe maker, pipers Graham Mulholland and Bill McLaughlan and Jo Ross, violin maker. Pete Clerk has made noted local appearances playing the Niel Gow fiddle from Blair Castle while Bill Baxter is a publisher of Scottish music. The singer, fiddler and composer, Dougie McLean, about whom a song was composed entitled 'Niel Gow's apprentice', has his recording studio overlooking the Dunkeld Bridge, while his bar provides a suitably relaxed setting for many traditional songs and tunes. One can only feel that if Niel Gow were to return today, despite the great physical alterations to his village of Inver and to both Dunkeld and Little Dunkeld, he would heartily approve of the continuing love of traditional music in the local populace and of their determination to nurture and further enrich the musical inheritance which he bequeathed them.

Inver

the village and its people

Inver meal mill showing sluice gates which directed the water to the meal mill and the sawmill as required. Charles McIntosh is seen on the right. [Perth Museum & Art Gallery]

Meal mills

From earliest times, the fast flowing River Braan has supplied a reliable source of water for the mills of Inver. This, along with its proximity to the West Ferry, was the reason for the rise of the village.

In the pre-reformation period Inver formed part of the Bishopric and rent from the mill and mill lands went to the upkeep of the manse and Chaplain of Inver. Mention is made in the *Atholl Muniments* of a waulk mill as well as 'mill and mill lands of Inver' acquired by the Robertsons of Lude in 1623.[1] When ownership passed to the Atholl family in 1683 their intent seems to have been to develop the mills. A proposal was made and costed for a lint mill in 1718 but there is no evidence from the rentals that it was ever built. The first tack of the mill lands given to Neill Stewart in 1735 mentions a saw mill, mill lands, acres and crofts at a rental of £666. 13s. 4d., a mill sow, six pigs and twelve poultry.[2]

The corn mill was by far the most important of these mills. Neill Stewart, the tenant, was expected to supply corn and straw for stabling the Duke's horses and grooms when passing through on their journeys north and south. The accounts show that the groom would stay at the coach house for a few nights at a time rather than the inn at the ferry, where stabling would be reserved for travellers. Further expansion took place in 1743 when Charles McGlashan acquired a nineteen year lease. He had been the miller at Ladywell but the Duke decided to have that mill demolished and the thirlage transferred to the mill of Inver. Mention is made in the Atholl Rentals of 1754 of a malt barn, a kiln and a coble (a vat for steeping malt) as well as a coach house.[3] Rent was also paid for two cottars houses for the under miller and servant.

The tenants of Inver, along with those of Ladywell, Little Dunkeld, Torrivald and Inchmagrannachan, were thirled to Inver mill, that is, they were bound to take their corn to be ground there. They also had certain obligations to help in the repairs to the mill, bring down new mill stones when required and keep the lade cleared. In addition, they had to pay the miller a proportion of their corn ground. These dues were termed multures.

All thought of expansion of the Inver mills ceased abruptly when Charles Edward Stuart landed in Moidart in 1745. James Duke of Atholl, a Hanoverian, fled Dunkeld leaving the ancestral home to his exiled elder brother Duke William who now returned with the Prince to fight for the Jacobite cause. This left the tenantry of Atholl in a quandary. Should they support Duke James or Duke William? Not surprisingly, the men of Dunkeld and Inver were reluctant to join the rebels and only four men from Inver and Little Dunkeld could be pressed into service. The local people were expected to provide meal for the troops as well as the prisoners held at Logierait. By February 1746 supplies were running low at Inver mill and when McGlashan was ordered to send meal to Blair Castle he protested:

> Please know that I have little or no meall sucken [meal paid as mill dues by cottars] and the little meall I get from them, it does not maintain my family; wherefore you'll be so good as to tell His Grace I have not a Boll by me, of what meall multure I got this winter. I have a few Bolls oats by me, which I intended for seed, and if I should meall them, my miller assures me that a Boll of them would not give three firlots meall.[4]

Notes on sketch of Inver 6 April 1830, in which the buildings which for improvement might be removed are coloured red.

Mr Graham, factor.

	No. 1	Old Boathouse—occupied by people employed at Saw Mills	
	2	Room adjoining do. occupied by Joseph Sim	*Stewart*
	3	A shed and byre vacant	*Grizel Farquharson*
	4	House occupied by Charles Conacher	
To remove to No. 12	5	**Thos. Gibson House & Weaving Shop**	} *Harris*
	6	} ~~Do Shed & Byre~~	}
	7	}	
To remove to No. 12	8	**Widow Menzies & Widow McLaren**	*A. Duff Smith*
	9	**John Bertram Barn** see No. 17	
	10	Charles Gibson Aberfeldy Post-House—see No. 13	
	11	Mrs Archer Sewing Schoolmistress	*J Robertson at Mill*
To remove	12	John Seaton *By Widows McLaren & McDougal*	
	13	Chas. Gibson Byre—see No. 10	*& Barn*
For mad woman	14	Chas. Scott, sublet by him to Grizel Farquharson. See Nos. 19, 31 & 32	*J. Duff's house*
	15	Chas. McIntosh house—see No. 20	*Widow McIntosh*
	16	**John Farquharson** *& Shop*	
	17	John Bertram House—see No. 9	
	18	William Borrie	
	19	**Chas. Scott Byre**—see Nos. 14, 31 & 32	*Js. Arthur & Shop*
	20	**Chas. McIntosh Byre**—see No. 15	*Jo. Duff Byre*
	21	Jas. McDonald Cartwright Shop	
	22	Do. House and Shop	*& C. McIntosh*
	23	**P. & J. Murray** **Byre**	
	24	**Do.** **Warping Mill**	
	25	Do. Houses & Weaving shop	
	26	Inn Stables *& cart shed*	
	27	**Part of inn ruinous**	
	28	} Do. Habitable	
	29	}	
Dye house for smith	30	Robt. Menzies Dyer	
	31	Chas. Scott **should be removed to accommodate Smith**	
	32	Do. **Wooden Shed**	
	33	Proposed new site for Smithy	
	34	**Old Kiln**	
	35	**Do. Meal Mill**	
	36	**Part of do. ruinous**	
	37	**Mrs Crerar's Wooden Shed**	
Widow Borrie Mercht. to go to new house	38	**Donald Borrie—might accommodate Saw Mill people**	
to go to new house	39	**Peter Low** **do.** **do.**	
mad woman to go to No. 30	40	**Alex. McDougal** **do.** **do.**	
	41	**Widow Duff** **ruinous** *may go to new house*	
	42	**Do. Byre** **do.**	
	43	**D. & A. Duff Weavers Shop do.**	
	44	**Wooden shed used as Smithy.**	

[Atholl Archives D4/12]

Bold print indicates that the words were written red ink, while italics indicate pencil notes in the original.

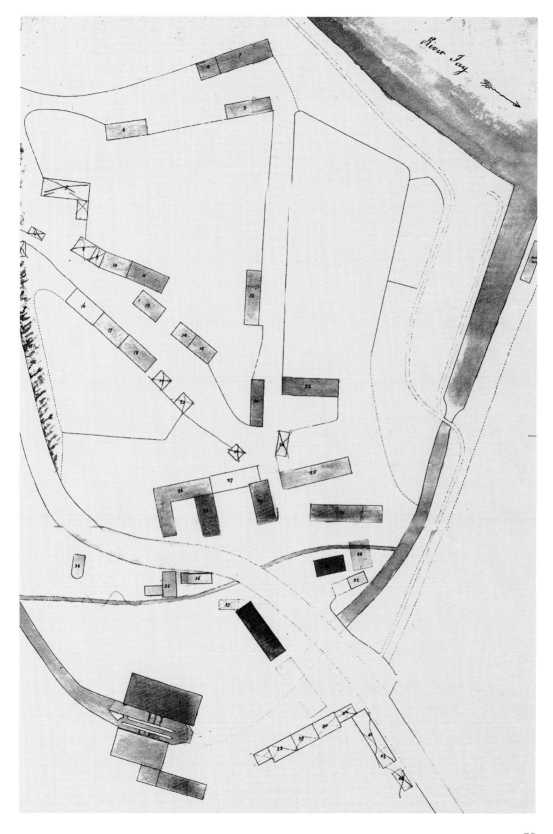

River Tay

75

No.	Name	Designation	No.	Name	Designation
1.	John Arthur		20.		Wood Shed
	Widow Crerar		21.	Chas. Macintosh	Musician
	John Kennedy	Sawmiller	22.	James Macdonald	Carpenter
2.	Widow Stewart		23.		Carpenter's Shop
3.		Fuel House	24.		Smithy
4.	John Stewart	Woodman	25.	John Robertson	Sawmiller
5.	Chas. Stewart	Sawmiller	26.	John Scott	Pauper
6.	do. do.	Byre	27.	David Thomson	Smith
7.	Donald Duff	Woodman	28.	Thomas Jackson	Innkeeper
8.	John Macdonald	Shop Carpenter	29.	do. do.	Inn
9.	John Macgregor	Woodman	30.	Mrs Borrie	Grocer
10.	James Robertson	Sawmiller	31.	do. do.	
11.	Alex. McDougal	Carpenter	32.	Hugh Robertson	Letter Carrier
12.	do. do.		33.	James Bell	Carpenter
13.	Betty Macintosh	Washerwoman	34.		Stable
14.	Widow Laird		35.		do.
15.	John Mcgregor,	Byre	36.		Sawmill
16.	Betty Fleming	Sempstress	37.	Meal Mill	
17.	Niel Gow's House		38.	Mrs Robertson	
18.	do. do.	Byre	39.	Wood shed	
19.	B. Macintosh,	Fuel House			

[A.A. D4/12]

Notes with plan of Inver 1861

Inver Meal Mill—James Robertson, Farmer

Cottages on ~~left hand~~ south side of public road.

	1.	J. McInnes—Electrician		XXXIII
x	2.	Robert Dow—retired Sawmiller	*Go out*	XXXII
x	3.&4.	James McDougall—retired	*ex watcher, 35 yrs. good man*	{XXX
			shop daughter	{XXXI

Cottages on right hand side of public road

1.	William & Peter Scott—Woodman	*outside men, about 50, sister*	XXIV
2.	John Stewart—estate labourer	*alright*	XXIII

The Square

1.	Mrs McIntyre—Widow	}	{
2.	Mrs/McIllrick—Widow	}*lodgings*	{XXIX
3.	Mrs Robertson—Widow		{

Cottages at foot of hill

1.	Charles McIntyre—Forester	*official house*	XXVI
2.	Duncan Seaton—Railway Surfaceman	*20 years*	XXV

Cottages on the hill

	1.	William Keir—sawmill labourer		VI
	2.	Miss Janet Stewart	*sister Charlie Stewart Craigvinean Cottage*	VIII
	3.	William Cramb—Boiler man at Creosote Tank		XVII
x	4.	John McIntosh—Estate labourer	*to be outed*	XIV
	5.	Mrs Cameron—Widow	*alright—Sandy Cameron's Widow*	XVIII
	6.	James Robertson—Woodman	*alright*	XIII
	7.	Woodmens Bothy	*out of order*	XX
	8.	Charles McIntosh—retired Postman	*alright*	XXI
good house	9.	James McDonald—, retired Joiner/Woods dept. Blair Atholl		
			the Clan	XXII
	10.	Mrs McDougall—Widow	*alright*	XI
		Hillside Cottage—John Scott—Postman	*Fiddler good*	IV
		Boat House—John McKay—Estate Joiner		I

[A.A.D4/12]   Italics indicate additional pencil notes.

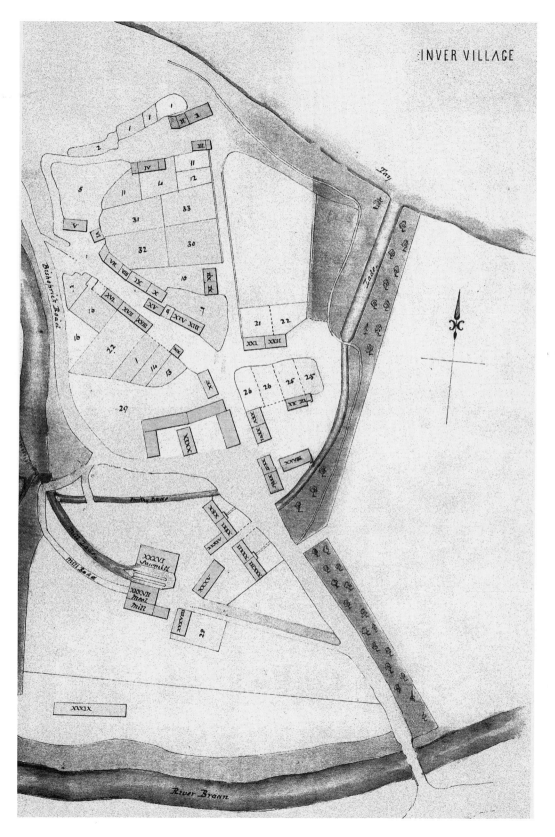

INVER VILLAGE

When Jacobite guards were stationed at the West Ferry, their officer ordered McGlashan and his wife Jean to pay the men silver money in exchange for the bank notes they had been paid. For this demeanour they were taken prisoner to Perth and charged with assisting the rebels.[5]

With the rout of the Jacobites at Culloden in 1746 and the return of Duke James, life resumed normality in Inver remarkably quickly. Two years later plans were afoot to expand the mills and the building of a new granary and girnal were well ahead. Considering the importance of the corn mill to the area, it is assumed that it was a stone built and slated building with a vertical paddle. John Shaw in his book *Water Power in Scotland* gives an excellent description of this type of mill.

It was to Charles McGlashan's mill that Niel Gow took his oats and bere to be ground. His acre of land gave him an ample supply of corn, for when the Duke offered him more land he assured His Grace that he had plenty, adding ' . . . the auld meal is never oot o' the girnal till the new's in it'.[6]

With the easing of the thirlage laws at the end of the eighteenth century, the tenants of Little Dunkeld were no longer obliged to take their oats to Inver. The estate were more interested in a lint mill in the eighteenth century and in erecting a sawmill in the early nineteenth century. The corn mill thus suffered neglect. Extensive repairs in carpentry and re-slating the roof were undertaken from 1810–1813 but despite this a report in 1822 stated, 'The meall mill at Invar [sic] with the kiln are in such a state as to require a considerable outlay'.[7] Crerar, the tenant, offered to pay part of the outlay of a new mill but nothing seems to have been done and the 1831 plan shows the corn mill and kiln in a ruinous condition. However, in the spring of 1831, Sir John Stewart, laird of Murthly, decided to demolish the corn mill at Little Dunkeld, thus leaving the way clear for another corn mill at Inver to serve the area. Furthermore, a new sawmill was being planned for Inver and it was decided to convert the old saw mill into a corn mill. For the first time, the corn mill was to be run independently of the inn, under the management of William Robertson. He built a three room house for himself, where he worked with two servants until his death in 1847.

He was succeeded by Alexander Robertson who was described in the 1851 census as a corn and flour miller, employing two millers. In 1874 this family acquired the farm land which had previously been part of the inn and they continued as millers until after 1909—sixty years service. After the Robertsons there was a succession of millers, the last of whom was Robert Ogilvie who came from Strathbraan. The Forestry Commission acquired the mill and park in 1948 and rented the mill and mill house to James McIntyre of Dunkeld who bought it from the Forestry Commission in 1951. The McIntyres worked the farm but in 1960 decided to develop a caravan park on the site by the River Braan on the field which in the eighteenth century was known as Will's Land. They also renovated and extended the mill house. This house still stands and is the home of James McIntyre's daughter and son-in-law. The kiln has almost disappeared now and, sadly, the mill is in a ruinous condition.

1. A.A. 22/10/4
2. Ibid., Rental 1735 7/420
3. Ibid., Rental 1745 7/418
4. Ibid., Jacobite Correspondence CCIX
5. Robert Scott Fittis, *Miscellanea Perthensis 1853–1861* page 5, number 2.
6. Sir Alexander Muir Mackenzie of Delvine, ed. *Tacketies and tyres in Strathbraan* (Perth, 1908) 13.
7. A.A. 68/12/331

Flax and waulk mills

The flooded river banks of the Braan and the Tay provided the ideal soil for the growing of flax. In earlier times it was grown in small quantities for domestic use but with the setting up of the Board of Trustees for Manufacturers in the 1720s great encouragement was given to raising it as a commercial crop to supply the growing linen industry. In spring the fields of blue flowers made a beautiful picture in Strathbraan and the Bishopric. Later, when the pea like seeds formed and the stalks were beginning to turn yellow, the crop was ready for harvesting. This at all stages was a laborious task. First, unlike corn, it was pulled up by the roots in handfuls. The bundles were left to dry for a few days before seeds were stripped off. The clean stalks, tied up in sheaves, were taken to the retting pool to be steeped. Evidence of dried up retting pools can still be seen on many farms. The steeping lasted two or three weeks and was a smelly process. Stones were put on top of the sheaves to keep them submerged and it was not unknown for gravestones to end up in the retting pond. These pools also made good hiding places for illicit goods.

When the outer fibres had become separated from the woody heart the stalks were carefully spread out to dry before being scutched, that is beaten with wooden mallets until the fibres were clean stripped. It was to ease the drudgery of scutching that lint mills were built in the eighteenth century but the initial process of feeding the flax into the rollers to break the stems was a dangerous job. After being rolled, the lint was taken to the loft above to be scutched until a fine fibre remained ready to be passed to the hecklers. Although the heckling was less arduous than the other processes, it was a highly skilled job. Itinerant hecklers often went round farms with their tools which consisted of a set of combs, through which the fibre was passed until it was fine enough for spinning. Because they worked in such a dusty, stoury atmosphere, hecklers were renowned for their drouthiness.

No doubt patches of flax were grown around Inver in the earlier part of the eighteenth century. Two stones of lint were part of the inventory of Margaret Young, the brewster's estate, and she was obliged to produce six hair of yarn as part of her rent. A hair consisted of 600 yards (548 metres) of spun yarn.

In 1748 the estate granted Charles McGlashan the park by the waterside for the growing of lint and the following year the Board of Trustees appointed him a flax raiser. Later that year the lint mill was in operation. McGlashan's mill was burnt down in November 1751, fire being a hazard common to lint mills. The Board of Trustees refused him funds to rebuild it, possibly because he hadn't insured it. But another mill was built and the report from the Stamp Master in 1772 informs us that there was enough water in the Braan to keep going throughout the year, that it broke the flax with rollers and scutched in the horizontal way, with the machinery in good condition and that it was 'clean scutched'. [1] It was worked by hired labourers for whom it was usually a winter job and hecklers were also hired. The Old Statistical Account of 1792 lists twenty three flax dressers in Little Dunkeld parish so there was no shortage of labour available. Andrew Duff, a later tenant, was granted £15 by the Board of Trustees in 1788 towards storage sheds. These were described in the O.S.A. as large, with slated roofs for storing unscutched flax.

The heyday of the linen industry in Little Dunkeld was the latter part of the eighteenth century.

By the turn of the century it was beginning to decline. The Board of Trustees reported that the quality of flax in the Bishopric was poor and production ceased in 1824. The flax dressers and scutchers, however, found alternative employment in the cotton mills of Stanley.

Waulking, or fulling, is the last process in making woollen cloth and has been done mechanically in waulk mills for centuries on the mainland of Scotland. In the islands it was until recently done communally by hand, or in some parts with the feet. Indeed the stamping movement, resembling the treading of feet, is the origin of the name waulking. The purpose of waulking was to mat together the warp and web threads of the woven cloth to shrink it. The cloth was first cut from the loom and taken to the mill where it was immersed in a trough of water. Next, the water was beaten out of the cloth by wooden blocks fixed at the end of hinged arms. This shrinking process left the cloth tight and waterproof.

There was a waulk mill in Inver at least from the seventeenth century and possibly before. It would be used by the tenants for finishing the cloth for domestic use as there is no evidence of woollen cloth being produced commercially in Little Dunkeld. The waulk mill was located further down the old lade from the corn mill on land now completely overgrown behind the two cottages on the east side of the road.

Patrick Murray became tenant of the waulk mill in 1729 along with 2 acres of the land called the Park and the Hempridge. His annual rent was £24 Scots for the mill, 6 hair of yarn and seven poultry. John Murray succeeded him in 1742, producing a tack for nineteen years for which he paid £24 Scots for the waulk mill, £16 for two acres of the Park and £2. 13s. 4d. for the Hempridge as well as seven poultry. [2] Thereafter, the waulk mill was operated by the Murray family until it was finally demolished in the early 1800s.

The dye house was sited alongside the waulk mill, a common practice, where water would be pumped from the lade. There the Murrays plied their highly skilled trade using vegetable dyes known to the Celts for generations.

The Rev. Alexander Irvine, minister of Little Dunkeld, writing in 1808 to the Rev. James Robertson, author of *General View of Agriculture in the County of Perth*, stated:

> But I am rather of the opinion that the ancient Caledonians used plants in dyeing as their descendents still continue to do; such as Heather, Water Lilly, Lady's Bed-grass, Bramble Shrub, perhaps some fruits such as Blackberries, besides Rock Moss or crotal, the bark of Aller (alder) and several other substances. [3]

Not much is written down about these early dyeing methods as the skills were handed down orally from one generation of a family to the next. Knowledge of which part of the plant to use and at what time of year to gather it, together with the best mordant to use for fixing the dye, was essential. If the wool was to be used for weaving tartan patterns then it would be dyed in hanks in smaller vessels but in the case of cloth, large copper vats were used. The dyer's expertise was in knowing how long to continue the dyeing process and ensuring that the wool was stirred to allow oxidisation. These skills were passed down through at least three generations of the Murray family until around 1810 when Robert Menzies took over. He carried on until 1830 when the dye house was demolished to make way for a new smiddy. Niel Gow, who started his life as a weaver, had a long connection with the Murrays, both as a customer and when Peter Murray played 'cello for him after his brother Donald died. Another musician customer was Charles Macintosh senior, who sent his linen yarn to be dyed blue prior to being woven into his patterned bed quilts. His wife also sent her hanks of wool to be dyed before being knitted up in socks or woven into the borders of blankets.

John Murray was the last of the family of dyers, his father having retired to property he acquired in Dunkeld. Peter and Thomas, another branch of the family, continued to work in Inver as weavers.

1. S.R.O. NG 1/19/1
2. A.A. Rental 1742 7/419
3. Rev. James Robertson *General View of the Agriculture of the County of Perth* (Perth 1831) 557.

Sketch of Blair Lint Mill (right) by Lady Emily Murray. [Blair Castle]

Sawmills and Planting

Throughout the eighteenth century, sawmilling in Inver was confined to producing wood for local use. The building of the lint mill, granary, stables, cottages and extension of the inn all created a demand for wood, in addition to cart wheels, ploughs and the ongoing repairs of buildings.

The natural woods of oak and birch around Inver and Ladywell supplied these needs. They were coppiced every twenty years or so by cutting them down to a few feet from the ground, leaving the stumps from which new growth sprouted, thus renewing the wood. It was from these woods that Niel's furniture was made when he set up house with Margaret in the 1750s. The oak bark supplied the Dunkeld tannery.

In the middle of the century John, the 4th Duke of Atholl, embarked on a programme of tree planting. He was eager to try out the value of larch, which had been introduced into Perthshire earlier in the century, as a commercial undertaking. The larch plantations thrived and experiments in their use in boat building with the new timber were successful. Two ferry boats were built, one of oak and one of larch, and it was the latter which proved to have the greater durability.

When, at the end of the eighteenth century, the plantations at Craigvinean, Ladywell and Inver were coming to maturity, it became necessary to erect a more powerful mill to replace the simple frame saws which had served the local need for so long. However, before a more powerful sawmill could be built, the water supply to drive it had to be increased. This entailed the construction of a new lade.

In November 1806 Robert Scott started the work of excavation to bring the water from the Braan to the mill. For this he was paid £104. 8s. An archway over the lade was made costing £52. 14s. 6d. The remains of the archway and the lade can still be seen. There is no reference in the accounts to the building of the two weirs on the Braan but this would probably be done in 1806 or 1829, when the lade was widened for yet another mill. Robert Scott was responsible for the actual building of the mill, which was of dressed stone and slated, which cost £443. 11s. The machinery consisted of eighteen vertical saws and one circular saw, the latter being one of the first such saws to be operated in any Scottish sawmill. James Fraser, the millwright in Dowally, installed the machinery and the Atholl accounts show that he was paid £113. 7s. 7d. for sundry repairs to Inver sawmill in 1810. This mill was in use until 1831 when it was converted to a cornmill and the machinery disposed of to the sawmill at Blair Atholl.

In 1829 Fraser entered into an agreement with the Duke of Atholl, to superintend all engineering work throughout his Perthshire estates, while the millwright was to remain free to continue his professional duties elsewhere. For this he was paid a salary of £75 per annum plus travel expenses over six miles from home and for which he had to produce plans and specifications free of charge.

James Fraser was one of those ingenious Scotsmen who lived out his life in obscurity, receiving little other than local recognition for all his inventions. He was born in Dowally, near Dunkeld, in 1782 and became a millwright of outstanding ability. In 1822 he adapted the principal of the Archimedes Screw and this was taken up by the Duke of Atholl for boats on the lochs on the estate. Fraser, however, received no credit for his invention as, slightly altered, it was taken up by another person. His next experiment was with a self propelling twin ferry boat. It consisted of two long narrow boats, lying parallel to each other and connected by a platform, constructed in such a way as to present the sides of the boats to the current of the river. A chain, stretched across the river and fixed to the platform, kept the boat on a straight course. It could carry four loaded carts with horses unyoked and it cost £200. This boat was first tried out in 1831 at Inver on the broadest part of the lade, a little above where it meets the Tay, much to the delight and consternation of the villagers. This time Fraser did receive recognition for his work, when he was presented with a medal from the Royal Society of Arts.

James Fraser was responsible for the second more powerful sawmill to be built at Inver. It had three vertical frames with twenty saws and three circular saws and it cost an estimated £1,533. The beautifully executed plans of this mill came into the possession of the Dunkeld and Birnam Historical Society in 1993 through the kindness of Mr Frederick Colby of Michigan, USA. His forbear, John Low, had emigrated from Inver around 1822 and was a friend of James Fraser. James Fraser died in 1854 and was buried in Dowally churchyard. His ferryboats long continued to ply on the Tummel and Tay at Logierait and Caputh while the sawmill at Inver operated for another hundred years and it is still standing today. James Fraser was succeeded by his nephew David Fraser who was the millwright at Tulliemet.

During the first half of the nineteenth century a variety of wood was produced at Inver. William Fleming was in charge of the overall forestry work in the area while James Borrie supervised the

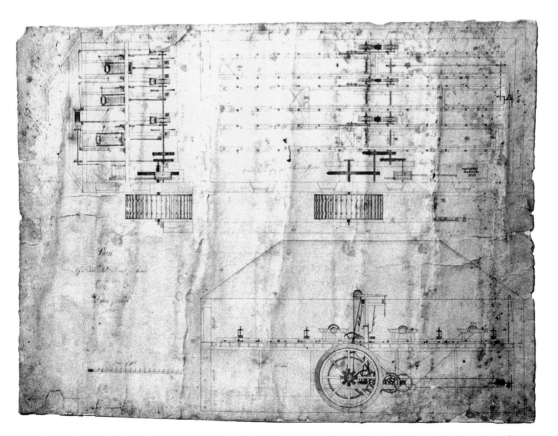

James Fraser's plan for a new sawmill at Inver, 1820. [Dunkeld & Birnam Historical Society]

cutting in the Inver area. The mill was run by the estate under the supervision of Malcolm MacCallum until 1825 when Alexander Robertson took over. In 1831 Robertson was responsible for organising the increased workforce for the more powerful new mill.

John Fleming, one of the first to work the new upright saws in Scotland, was in charge of the new mill. There were seven sawyers under him each as well as one man to work the horses, each man being paid two shillings per day. Some of the men were housed in the old boathouse while others occupied new houses built for them. A new smiddy was also built. Larch boards, oak, beech and lime were all cut and sold at Inver. Later, in 1839 when James Brodie took over the running of the mill, he supplied sleepers for the new railways which were being built. He paid his men ten shillings a week as carters, taking the timber to Perth. From there it was shipped to England.

While full time sawyers were turning out timber for ships and railways, up in the woods at Ladywell local casual labour was employed felling trees with cross cut saws and taking them to the nearby saw pit to be made into fencing and hurdles. Some of the timber cut at Ladywell was used to bottom the new toll road being built through Strathbraan while thinnings were used for burning charcoal on the west side of the Braan, opposite the Hermitage. With the decline of the linen trade weavers had to be prepared to turn their hand to what work they could get and were glad to take work in the woods.

As well as transporting sleepers to Perth by cart, timber was also floated down the Tay, although protests by Lords Kinnaird and Gray that this damaged the salmon fishing may have ended this practice. James Stewart, the Dunkeld poet, mentions engaging in conversation a man in charge of a floating raft near Inver and having his pocket picked for his friendliness.

The completion of the Perth to Dunkeld railway in 1856 and the consequent building of the village of Birnam created a local demand for timber. A number of Inver tradesmen obtained feus and built property in the new village. Then, in the early 1860s the railway was extended to Inverness, causing upheaval in Inver as the new line cut through the park land. This led to the expansion of Inver and a further demand for wood.

The census records throughout the nineteenth century show that steady employment as sawyers, woodmen and carters was given not only to local men such as Charles Macintosh but also to young men from further afield who were prepared to come to work, marry and start a family in the village. The accounts also show evidence of steady employment. For the years 1863–4 the wages bill for the wood foresters was £1,029. 12s. 51/2d. and the money owed to carpenters et cetera was £5,969. 10s. The highest woods sales recorded was £8750 in 1867. [1]

In 1860 John MacGregor was appointed to take charge of the estate woods and in 1868 land at Ladywell farm was converted into a nursery under his direction. This gave employment to men cutting broom to be used for thatching and also in tree planting. Women were employed to gather seed. The accounts show MacGregor himself being paid £100 for a half year plus £15 for keep of riding horse; £4. 7s. 6d. travelling expenses; £5. 17s. 6d. for services of clerk; £12. 10s. for keep of work horse, and a woodmen's pay bill at Ladywell of £49. 11s. [2] John Macgregor died 12 January 1892. He was succeeded by David Keir.

At this time the new smiddy, erected in the 1830s to replace the old wooden one, was kept busy making axe heads, sharpening axes, making broom hooks, nails, picks, hammers, hinges for palings and grates for the new houses.

Towards the end of the nineteenth century Inver mill continued turning out oak and larch pit props, supplying the needs of local joiners, especially those who were engaged in house building in the new village of Birnam and meeting the continuous demand for fencing. The 1891 census shows sixteen men in the village employed either in forestry or sawmilling.

Charles Macintosh, who as a young sawmiller lost all the fingers and thumb of his left hand in a tragic accident with a saw, was a knowledgeable botanist. During the latter part of the nineteenth century he observed the disastrous effect that aphids (insects) were having on the larch trees, causing the resin to bleed and the death of many trees. So great was the scourge that for a time at the turn of the century larch planting in the Atholl woods was suspended. When the disease was at its worst, flocks of great tits, blue tits and coal tits descended on the woods to feast on the insects in the winter months. It was the activities of the birds which finally conquered the menace of the aphis. Charles was also responsible for drawing attention to the unusual larch seedlings at the Ladywell nursery which proved to be a natural cross between the European larch and the Japanese. [3] When matured, the hybrid proved to have the best characteristics of both parents.

Forestry work on the Atholl estate, as well as giving much needed employment, benefited the whole community. David Keir, the head forester, wrote to the Duke in 1907 expressing the grateful thanks of the workmen employed in the woods for the handsome clubroom which had been laid out in the west wing of Inver inn. Here the local people could enjoy a game of cards or meet for a chat until it was finally incorporated into a dwelling house in the 1930s. [4]

The Atholl woods, along with those of neighbouring Murthly estate, provided the local folk with an endless supply of fuel. Going to the woods for a 'burden' was an almost daily exercise which Millais commemorated in his painting 'Winter Fuel' and James Macintosh, brother of Charlie, caught so perfectly in a photograph at the beginning of the century.

Mary Crerar recalls:

> As children, in the holidays and on Saturdays, we went to the woods as often as we could with bogies to gather chips and snedded pieces of branches and loved to hear the singing saws. The crash of falling timber was sad and terrifying at the same time. There were no power saws in those days, only the beautiful long cross cut saws of the best steel, with a man at each end pulling in rhythm. The better the steel, the more the saw 'sang'—a lovely sound. [5]

She goes on to describe an expedition to Inver park where she and her cousin, equipped with small axes, made a canoe out of a newly felled tree, only to have it confiscated by the foresters.

World War I saw the invasion by over three hundred men of the Newfoundland Forestry Corps who were employed to fell timber on Craigvinean. They were housed in huts at the foot of the hill and they had their own sawmill. A timber chute 3,200 feet in length delivered the timber by gravity to within a few yards of the mill. [6] It was some of the Newfoundlanders who recovered the bodies of the lady forestry workers who drowned in the Tay in the summer of 1918. The girls were employed at the Ladywell nursery and housed at the Inver Inn. Lady Dorothea writing to her brother Hamish in 1917 noted, 'Craigvinean wood down, cut by the Newfoundlanders, assisted by women who are also doing a great deal of agricultural work in Dunkeld'. [7] In 1918 Lord Tullibardine wrote to Lord James that, 'Craigvinean was sold to the government and brought in £43,000. All Ladywell woods etc. remain. We have a female squad at the nursery who, when they are not squabbling, work well.' [8]

After the First World War the financial circumstances of the Atholl Estate deteriorated to the point by which in 1932 a private company was formed under the title Atholl Properties Limited.

After protracted negotiations the company sold Craigvinean and part of Ladywell to the Forestry Commission in 1937 and a ten year plan of replanting to regenerate the denuded woods was undertaken on the rest of the estate. This was accomplished by the joint efforts of the estate, the Forestry Commission's Woodland Dedication Scheme and the Scottish Woodland Owners Association.

In 1942 the Duchess of Atholl presented the Hermitage to the National Trust for Scotland in memory of her husband, the 8th Duke of Atholl and it now attracts visitors all year round, unlike former times when early travellers were obliged to seek the services of a guide.

In latter years forestry work has undergone a revolution. The singing saws so beloved of Mary Crerar gave way to the rasping chain saws in the 1960s. At first they were very unpopular because they were clumsy and awkward to handle but later models were lighter and they soon came to be in general use. Thirty years on and the chain saws have themselves been replaced. Nowadays one man sitting in a cabin with a crane and a processing head at the end of it can fell a tree, cut it to the right length, trim the branches off and stack the timber. This has led to a drastic reduction in the number of forestry workers. [9]

Gone too are the horses employed in dragging the timber, although horses are making a welcome comeback in sensitive recreational areas where it was found that the crawler tractors were doing too much damage. Nowadays, after centuries of bustle, the Inver inn stables lie silent and empty, giving no hint of former activity. Inver Park, where once the villagers grazed their cows and was later the scene of Scottish Horse camps, is now planted with fir trees and Christmas trees. Behind the Christmas trees are the offices of Tayside Enterprise Forestry which has replaced the Forestry Commission. They employ around forty-six people, comprising forest management, office staff, mechanical engineering and workshop personnel who between them cover a wide area stretching to Rannoch Moor, Loch Tay, Kirkmichael, the north Angus glens, Dundee and north Fife. Thus two hundred years of woodland management is being kept alive in Inver.

If the stables lie empty, it is pleasing to know that the old saw mill building is a hub of activity. Here Mrs Jean Burhouse makes and repairs high quality furniture. In 1953 Mr Hendry the head forester, had reported:

> The existing estate sawmill is located at Inver. The building is at least 100 years old and much of the driving machinery is of a like age. The power is by a large, overshot water wheel and by metal and timber cog wheel transfer to the main shaft. Due to wear and tear the unit will eventually become uneconomic, repair work is expensive, moreover during the continued dry spell the water supply from the River Braan becomes too low to maintain an efficient power unit. The site at Inver is much too small for stocking purposes which in itself debars consideration of replacement with a modern plant. [10]

Then in a letter to Mrs Campbell Preston dated 26 January 1956, Mr Stewart, the Factor, stated, 'The existing mill is now being worked where possible by a tractor, as the main flywheel and water wheel literally disintegrated yesterday morning'. [11] The Hydro Board was contracted and by the end of the first week of 1957 electricity was installed enabling the mill to keep in production until the new mill was ready at Spoutwells Dunkeld and the machinery disposed of. Thus ended James Fraser's pioneering mill.

Jean Burhouse moved into the sawmill in 1985. The larch slat fencing that had been produced there latterly was no longer profitable owing to competition from the mass produced market. Jean was told she could have the mill provided she cleared it out. In an interview, she described the scene that confronted her:

> Inside, it was just as if people had left the day before—there were a few bits of machinery, sawdust on the floor, bits of odd wood—everything except tools. At the back of the workshop there were two big tanks where they dipped the fencing in creosote. It was knee deep at the back in creosote sawdust—we burnt some of it.

There was a kiln where the sawdust was burnt. The chimney still stands.

Before the kiln was erected, the sawdust was piled up in bins at various points in the village, the main one was at the side of the Braan, into which much of it was tipped. No questions were asked about pollution in those days but then there was an excellent flow of water due to the two substantial croys built of wooden planks and stones further upstream.

When Jock Robertson told me that horses were sometimes buried in the sawdust bings instead of being taken to the knackers yard, I thought he was having me on. But Bill Edwards confirmed that this was true. The hardest bit was getting the beast out of the stable and as a child he acted as chief mourner. Horses were an endless source of interest to the Inver boys.

The drying shed still stands, lying parallel to the river so that the moisture laden air went through the shed ensuring that the timber didn't dry out too quickly, causing the wood to crack. It would thus take a year to dry out. They had no need of kiln-dried timber.

Jean and her husband Graham worked tirelessly to set up their workshop. Now they have a thriving business employing five people, producing custom built furniture and undertaking restoration work.

It is good to see the old building still a hub of activity.

1. A.A. Bundle 148.
2. Ibid., Bundle 149.
3. E. Cox, ed. *Dunkeld Remembered* (Dunkeld, 1993) 17 & 35.
4. J. Anderson, *Chronicles of the Atholl and Tullibardine Families VI* (Aberdeen, 1991) 9.
5. E. Cox, ed. *Dunkeld Remembered* (Dunkeld, 1993) 35.
6. *Perthshire Advertiser* 26 Dec. 1917
7. J. Anderson, *Chronicles of the Atholl and Tullibardine Families VI* (Aberdeen, 1991) 105.
8. Ibid., 110
9. Information kindly supplied by the Forestry Commission, Inver
10. J. Anderson, *Chronicles of the Atholl and Tullibardine Families VI* (Aberdeen, 1991) 418.
11. Ibid., 431

Marble mill at Inver

In 1829, following the decision to erect a new sawmill at Inver, it was proposed to convert the current sawmill into a stonemill [1] to cut and polish the marble which had been quarried at Glen Tilt since 1815.

James Fraser, millwright Dowally, was commissioned to undertake the work which was proceeded with between August 1829 and September the following year. With his usual ingenuity Fraser devised a machine for sawing the marble and sliding frames for polishing. The cost of erecting the sawmill was £112. 15s. and for the polishing mill £90. 11s. 2d. By 20 June the sawmill seems to have been in operation when a man was paid 10s. 6d. for three and a half days sawing marble. Thereafter no further reference has come to light of any workmen's wages. James Fraser submitted his account on 29 September 1830. A note at the foot of the account for the polishing mill states that the building was stopped on 30 September 1830, the date of the death of the Duke.

It is a matter of speculation if the cause of the sudden cessation of the work was an act of panic caused by the death of His Grace or whether it was abandoned because by this time foreign imports of marble had greatly reduced the viability of the venture. Eventually the machinery of the old sawmill was sold off to Blair Atholl to be used in the new sawmill there. What happened to James Fraser's machinery for processing the marble is not known.

1 A.A. 69/5/363

Account for marble production. [Blair Castle]

Tradesmen

It is difficult to assess how many tradesmen, and what craft they practised, were living in Inver in the first part of the eighteenth century. The rentals do not list the people living in the cottar houses until 1754 and even then some of the estate workers would be living rent free with some paying rent to the innkeepers who had cottages for their workers from the estate. There would certainly be one or possibly two millers, one performing the function of mill wright as well. Although no smith is named until 1754, a smiddy would be necessary to attend to the shoeing of horses in addition to making tradesmens' implements and iron items for domestic use.

The situation becomes clearer with later rentals naming tenants, the parish records naming tradesmen employed by the kirk session and the accounts recording sums paid to the workmen. But the picture is still incomplete as the parish register records births to parents not mentioned elsewhere: likewise roup sales list such tradesmen purchasing items. This was the situation until full details of those employed were recorded in the census records from 1841–1891, the estate census of 1831, 1861 and 1909, with further information from the valuation rolls 1855–1992 and oral evidence from former and present inhabitants.

Alexander Stewart, shoemaker. [C McBeath]

Millwrights

We know from the rentals of 1754 that Charles McGlashan, tenant of the inn and mills, had two cottar houses for his under-millers. The first of these that we know of was John Lesley, who came to Inver in the 1760s and settled down with his bride in a cottage near to Niel Gow. The mills of that period were of such a simple construction, made mostly of wood, that their maintenance could be undertaken by the miller, with the help of the wright and the blacksmith for such iron parts as there were. The wooden cog wheels required constant attention as the parts rotted with the pressure of the water. Later in the century, when Alexander McGlashan acquired the tenancy of the inn and mills, a point in his favour was the fact that his brother John was a mill wright.

After Niel's death in 1807, John Bartrum, millwright, occupied his cottage. By that time a new saw mill had been built by James Fraser, who also certainly undertook some repairs, but most of Bartrum's work would be keeping the corn mill and lint mill in good order. Fraser, whose career has been mentioned in connection with the construction of the saw mill, took over complete supervision of the mills in 1829 and Bartrum was employed under Brodie working in the woods. He was the last mill wright resident in Inver. He took over Niel's acre of land as well as his cottage and worked the land with a spade, which suggests that he was of Irish origin. The 1841 census states he was not born in Scotland. His wife Lucky seems to have been a character. She did not trust the local miller and preferred to travel the few miles up Strathbraan to Ballinloan mill to have her puckle corn ground there. Like her neighbour, Mrs Farquharson, she had the Scriptures at her finger tips and was ever ready with an apt Biblical quotation. John Bartrum died an octogenarian in 1847 and Lucky in 1854. Thereafter, Niel's house gradually sank into a state of disrepair.

Opposite:
Tradesmen at Birnam Coach Works, 1889.
Left to Right: *Joseph Sim, blacksmith, holding fore-hammer; Alex McIntosh with spoke dog;*
A. Hutton, joiner, with plane; A. McIntyre with ball peined hammer;
George Goble with axle steel; H. McIntyre; Tom Goble, wheelwright; Tom Low, joiner;
John Sim, coach-builder; Peter Watson with felloe of ash wood.

[Eileen Cox]

Cartwrights

When the young Niel Gow, along with the other lads, went to Birnam Hill to cut peats and divots, they brought sods home on sledges or slipes drawn by a pony. Those Inver cottars possessing carts were obliged to go to Perth, taking with them yarn or anything they might have to sell and returning with coal for the laird. These goods were carried on small primitive carts made of birch frames, and solid wooden wheels with a hole in the middle to take the birch wood axle-tree. These aptly name tumbrils, with their tumbling motion, could be made up by the village joiner. With the improved turnpike roads came the demand for better carts, with better horses to draw them. This in turn required highly skilled craftsmen to make them. The MacDonald family, known as 'The Clan', who came to Inver around 1790, supplied that need.

There were by now two kinds of cart in use, the long cart used for hay and harvest, the other type, the coup cart, which could be tipped up to empty any kind of load such as fuel or dung. The old solid wood wheels were replaced by the beautifully crafted spoke-wheels. These were made of well seasoned ash wood, the spokes carefully shaped with the spoke shave, the lighter the better, making less weight for the horse to carry. The rim of the wheels consisted of arc shaped sections called felloes, each accurately drilled to take two spokes. The nave was made of elm and the axle of

iron. At each stage a high degree of accuracy was required and when this joiner work was completed the whole wheel was taken to the nearby smithy to be ringed.

The smiths first job was to measure the circumference of the wheel with a traveller, then cut a long strip of iron to the correct length, forked at each end. This was heated on the red hot fire, then taken to the anvil where it was hammered to make a ring that would fit the wheel entirely. Next came the most exciting part, when the wheel was placed on the platform on the ground and the red hot metal band, gripped with tongs by four or five workmen, was dropped on the wheel. Woe betide the joiner who had made the wheel the wrong size, or the smith who hadn't heated the rim to the correct intensity. Buckets of water from the nearby lade, thrown over the wheel, made the rim contract so it gripped so tightly that it would last for years. [1] Understandably, wheels were highly valued possessions and a farmer might have two pairs which he could fit to the body of whichever cart he required.

The Macdonalds were at one time the only cartwrights between Inver and Kingussie. The 1851 census shows them employing three men. They were a Gaelic speaking family, hailing from the parish of Dull. Charlie McIntosh, who lived next door to them, described the men as 'not tall and of thick set build' and by all accounts the kind of characters who attracted legends.

One night, having over indulged in the inn, MacDonald became aggressive, issuing a challenge to a sword fight to the inoffensive 'Clearach More' (Big Clerk). Next morning MacDonald, armed with his sword, crossed in the ferry to Dunkeld and made for the house of the hapless clerk who had completely forgotten the challenge. The furious Highlander, baulked of his sport, built a cairn, dubbing it Cowards Cairn.

James, the last man of his clan, inherited the family skills, producing as well as carts fine furniture, tables, chairs and dressers. Unmarried, he was looked after most of his life by his sister Isabel. When he lay dying, the minister and a few neighbours came to watch by his bedside, as was the custom in those days. To help them keep awake, they brewed themselves a pot of tea.

'Dinna worry, James,' the minister said, 'We've brought our own tea and sugar and milk.'

'Aye,' quipped the dying man 'but it's no' yer own coal.' [2]

Thus ended the reign in Inver of the famous 'Clan'.

1. Related by the late Hugh Sim, Birnam, in conversation with H.J.
2. As told to H.J. by Mrs Peg Malloch, formerly resident in Inver.

Blacksmiths

The estate plan of Inver 1830 shows the smiddy as a wooden building situated on the smiddy lade. The first mention of a smith in the rentals is 1754 although there must have been one long before that. The mill's equipment would be limited to a forge, an anvil, vice, bellows, hammers and files, enough for the smith to shoe the estate horses and those of the travellers on their way to and from the ferry. Another demand for his services was the miller who would rely on him to mend or replace iron parts of the mill stones and wheels, and from the other tradesmen to repair or mend their tools.

John Gow, alias McIntosh, possibly a brother of Niel, is the first smith named in the rentals. In 1754 he produced a life rent tack of a house and yard, paying yearly twelve pounds Scots, six poultry and six dargs. He was granted a license to sell ale by the Commissioners of Supply in 1753, which suggests that he was working as a smith sometime before he acquired the tack. Andrew Gow, possibly a younger brother, also a smith, had a house for which he paid £1. 1s. per year. He enlisted in 1762, no doubt to escape his debtors. A recruiting party had descended on Dunkeld, 'enrolling men of all sizes and all ages from fourteen years to four score years'. [1] Andrew was made a sergeant, but was in debt for the recruiting money. He married Elspeth Ealdge, the last of an old Dunkeld family from whom she inherited Castle Clearach. She lost her inheritance when Andrew pledged the property to Niel Gow in 1767 as security for a bond. Niel foreclosed the bond, securing the property which he sold in 1775, after which there is no further reference to Andrew and Elspeth. The smiddy was carried on by John McIntosh until 1810.

Alexander Duff, who succeeded him, saw many changes. The improved turnpike roads demanded improved carts and coaches to travel on them, demanding highly proficient smith work. The new sawmill also required proficient work that could no longer be undertaken by the miller, while in agriculture the improved plough, with its iron coulter replacing the old Scotch plough, also created more work for the local smiddy. The accounts show payments to the smith for hammers, nails, broomhooks and axes, mostly supplied to the woodmen. The old wooden smiddy was no longer able to cope with the increase in work so it was replaced in 1837 with another, built beside the new lade and, essentially, near James McDonald the cartwright.

After Alexander Duff retired in 1840 there was a succession of smiths, the last of whom was David Thomson. The new houses being built had grates instead of the open hearths of the old cottages. Palings were replacing the old dykes while the increasing forestry work created a constant demand for tools. A smiddy and a coachworks was built in the new village of Birnam in 1856. Thereafter, smith work was either carried out there or at Dunkeld. When David Thomson moved to Broughty Ferry, no smith replaced him. Later cottages were built on the site of the Inver smiddy and all trace of it and its activity has entirely disappeared.

It has been observed many time that the smiddy was usually the focal point of village life. This does not seem to have been the case in Inver, where, until it too closed its doors in the 1860s, the centre of village life was the inn, and the dominant personality the innkeeper.

---

1   J. Stewart Murray, 7th Duke of Atholl Chronicles of the Atholl and Tulliebardine Families
     Vol. III (Edinburgh 1908) 493

John Farquharson—Spinning wheel maker

Although John Farquharson is described in the 1841 census as a wheel wright he in fact made spinning wheels, earning him the nickname of Wheelie Farquharson. He came from Grantully to Inver in the 1820s when weaving was still an important trade.

In the eighteenth century the simple muckle wheel or wool wheel was much in use, as the roup sales record. Although they were called wool wheels, they were also used for spinning flax. These simple wheels could be made by the local joiners but the improved two flyer spinning wheels required the skill of a first class wood turner. Perthshire was in the forefront of this craft. Duchess Jane, wife of the 4th Duke of Atholl, encouraged Peter Squires to invent a two flyer wheel which enabled the women to greatly increase their output. As the minister noted in the Little Dunkeld Old Statistical Account in 1794:

> Of late, spinning wheels with two flies have become pretty frequent, with which women spin nearly twice as much as with the wheels of one fly.— Some young women, without any previous teaching, are able to spin so fine a thread as $3^1/_2$ spindles [1] from the lb. avoirdupois. [2]

The craft of spinning wheel maker was therefore well established in the area when John Farquharson set up shop next door to John Bartrum the mill wright. During the days, his wife Ellen cleared the furniture in one of the rooms to make way for her young pupils who arrived with their little stools, ready to receive instruction in sewing and no doubt spinning.

After the 1830s the weaving industry declined, killed by the cotton trade. Although women continued to spin for their own satisfaction, they were no longer able to pay the rent from it. With the improved roads and transport the area was attracting tourists, many of whom made their way to the nearby Hermitage. John Farquharson set up his stall at the entrance gate and there sold quaichs, egg cups, pincushions, stands and toddy ladles, which he turned on his lathe instead of the bobbins and the spinning wheels. His wife Ellen died in 1854 and a year or two later John moved to Grantully where his son Donald was a gardener and there he died in 1875. He lies buried in Grantully churchyard.

1. By the end of the eighteenth century a spindle was 14,4000 yards of linen yarn.
2. O.S.A. Vol. VI 410.

Weavers

Leezie Gow spun the yarn
John Morrow dyed it,
Charlie the weaver wrocht the claith
And Jamie Joar sewed it. [1]

Inver, situated in a flax growing, sheep rearing, area with its lint mill, waulk mill, warping mill and dye house was the ideal place for the hand loom weaver to ply his trade. Niel Gow, according to Joseph McGregor, was a plaid weaver, that is he wove the grey homespun cloth worn by the ordinary folks, although he himself is always portrayed as dressed in tartan. Even as late as 1767 he was designated weaver and musician, although by then playing was occupying much more of his time.

The Murray family, who came to Inver in the 1750s, were foremost in the trade in Inver, with their dye houses and waulkmills for woollens and their warping mill and weaving shop for linen production. They were followed closely by Charlie Macintosh in the 1780s. He had two looms in his house and a warping mill in his loft, the looms paid for by the Board of Trade and Agriculture, the Duke of Atholl being a trustee of the Board. As early as 1735 the trustees were offering to send trained journeymen to Dunkeld to help the weavers there to improve the quality of their work and a Stamp Master was appointed to stamp the linen that reached the desired standard.

There were two systems by which a handloom weaver could sell his wares, the putting out system and the customer weaver. In the putting out system the manufacturer supplied the weaver with the yarn and returned to collect the completed webs and pay the weaver. By contrast, the customer weaver procured his own yarn, wove it and sold it to private houses who might commission it, or sold it at market. There were also in Little Dunkeld two manufacturers employing in all ten weavers, one at Burnside owned by Robert Dow, the other at Inchewan owned by William Harris.

The Inver people seemed to operate on the customer system. Charles Macintosh describes how his grandfather and father either sold their fine linen sheets, towels and quilted bed covers to farms or big houses, or took them to Dunkeld market. Other weavers also took their pieces in carts to Dunkeld where they had to be stamped, their measuring sticks checked on the ell on the wall to ensure their accuracy, and finally sold to customers. In the Old Statistical Account for Little Dunkeld mention is made of weavers purchasing yarn from hawkers, then making it into webs of green cloth. There were at that time 160 weavers in the parish operating under these various systems. Weaving involved the whole family, the children, the women and the girls spinning, the children winding the spun yarn on the pirns or measuring it on the winding wheel. The tedious, highly skilled task of setting up the warp was thankfully left to either the Macintoshes or the Murrays, who had the warping mills. The writer of the New Statistical Account records that the linen industry had declined in Little Dunkeld, unable to compete with the new cotton industry. Some weavers found work in the Stanley Mills while others turned to forestry work and saw milling. The McIntoshes and the Murrays were already established as musicians, although Charlie records that his father still did some weaving until the middle of the century. Instead of the clack of the looms, the whine of the sawmill combined with the sound of the fiddle in Inver.

1. Sir Alexander Muir Mackenzie of Delvine, ed. *Tacketies and tyres in Strathbraan* (Perth, 1908), 8.
    John Morrow was Murray the dyer, Charlie Macintosh was the weaver while Jamie Joar was Dewer, Whip the Cat. All were Inver residents

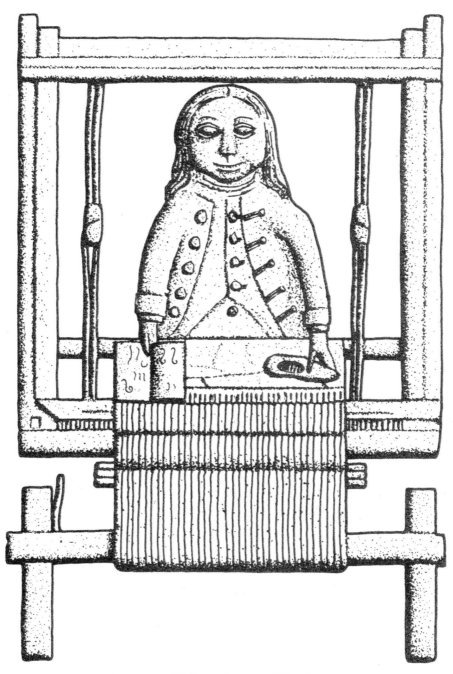

A weaver at his loom, from an old headstone.

Shoemakers

My faither is a cordiner
Maks strang buits and shaes,
But we maun wear bauchles
Maist o' the days.

From 'The Bairns' by Willie Soutar.

The oak woods around Inver supplied bark for the tannery in Dunkeld which in turn provided the leather for the cordiners. Inver in the eighteenth century had two families of shoemakers, the Gibsons and the Duffs.

Shoemakers were sometimes known as cordiners or soutars, denoting that they had served an apprenticeship. There was a Cordiners Society in Dunkeld into which shoemakers in the area paid 10s. 6d. entry money, thereafter 6d. a quarter. The society paid 3s. weekly to those who were sick or too old to work and £1. 1s. towards the funeral expenses of each member. A cobbler had not completed a full apprenticeship, confining his work to mending shoes.

Women in the eighteenth century and into the nineteenth century went barefoot, keeping their shoes for church on Sunday, or infrequent visits to town. They cost 4s. a pair. The men required stout shoes for rough walking. These were of the brogue type with tongue and buckle. Shoes with ties came into fashion around 1790.

John Duff came to Inver in the late 1760s. He first appears in the rentals in 1774, paying £1. 10s. for a house and an acre of land. By 1800 he had two acres from which to supplement his income. He most probably supplied Niel with shoes. Considering the frequent journeys Niel made to Perth and Edinburgh, Cupar and Crieff, to mention but a fraction of the places he visited on foot, he must have been a good customer. John died in 1803 aged 72, leaving his widow Margaret to carry on the pendicle.

Charles Gibson first appears in the rental in 1799. He too had a pendicle as well as a byre and pasture for a cow. The right of pasturing a cow was a common source of dissent among the villagers and Charles had such a dispute for which he appeared before the minister who forbade him communion. A communion token was given to those entitled to attend, and his daughter Anne gave her father hers, which he presented at the communion table, but the Reverend Robert Allan had him removed.

Once the Dunkeld bridge was completed, shops there could supply the Inver people either with ready made shoes or shoes made to measure. When there was no longer any demand for his services, Charles became a postman delivering letters between Dunkeld and Aberfeldy, living to a ripe old age. Right into this century, some customers preferred to have their shoes and boots hand made, keeping the shoemakers in Dunkeld and Birnam in business. In 1912 there were three shoemakers in Dunkeld, two in Birnam and one in Trochry. Now people have to travel to Perth or Aberfeldy for their footwear.

Tinsmiths

The 1881 census for Inver lists two families of travelling tin smiths camping in Inver woods; John McKenzie from Kincardineshire and Robert Reid from Blair Atholl. Although they do not appear in earlier census records, we know from other sources that they frequented the area long before this. The Rev. John McMillan, the first minister of the newly erected St Mary's Episcopal church in Birnam, seems to have been kindly disposed to travelling families, for they came from far and near to have him join them in matrimony or baptize their children in the 1860s. Likewise, the Rev. J.S. Mackenzie, minister of Little Dunkeld parish, was equally popular with them as was his successor the Rev. Roger Gillies. Indeed, there is an area of Little Dunkeld churchyard where many of those travelling folk lie buried, with white wooden crosses to mark their graves.

In earlier times these travellers had been skilled in working silver, fashioning buckles for shoes or clasps for plaids. As fashions changed, they confined their skill to melting down silver or gold brought to them to be worked into brooches or rings.

They are best remembered, however, as tinsmiths, ready to mend pots and pans at cottage doors. The travellers camped at Inver wood, however, also supplied the local folk with new pans, milk cans, watering cans and all sorts of tin ware. The late Sandy Stewart leaves a clear description of how his uncle went about it:

> Fer makkin the tin ye needit a tinsmith's stake. . . . Hit wes like a letter 'T' an ye got them wae three or four wee neeks on the tap. Ye stuck hit in the grun in front o'ye an sat flat-leggit. The wan that the blacksmith hes is bigger an hit sits ontae the flair o' the smiddie. Then ye needit a wuidden mellet, hemmers, rivets fer pitten lugs on yer can, an snaps' fer cutin the shapes o yer tin. If ye were stuck fer solder ye could run it aff auld tins an this done fer yer seam. An ye hed whit thay cad spirit o salts and roset, the same as whit ye pit ontae a fiddle. When ye walt the seam, ye could rub the roset along yer seam. Ye could send fer tin tae Glesgae at that time an ye got big webs o tin. An if ye were short o tin, ye usetae get square boxes that ye got in bakersie shops fer hoddin cream or somethin. They had a screw-on lid an ye could open them oot an wash ae thae boxes oot, if ye were stuck fer tin. Ye could mak cans or oniething oot o the like o that. [1]

Cheap imports from abroad in the 1890s, plus easier accessibility to ironmongers shops by the rural population, decreased the demand for the travelling tinsmith's wares. He had to find other means of employment. The Inver wood camp, situated on the banks of the Tay with its beds of mussels, was ideally placed for pearl fishing. If in shallow water, this could be done by wading in, but working deeper water required a boat. The local joiner could make a pearl-boat for ten shillings (fifty pence) but Sandy Stewart preferred to put one together himself. He explains how:

> I made yin frae canvas. I got a big thing like a crate—Oh it was a big size o a thing, an afore I pit the canvas on, I tarred the box first. Then efter I, Ah tarred it, Ah pit the sail ontae hit when the tar was safe. Then right ower the tap o the sail-cover Ah taen they

big tacks, like slate tacks except they wes longer. Ah nailed them on tae the tar again an went ower the tap o the canvas again. Ah've seen three o us intae hit fer we made a set wae wuid at each side o hit. But if ye wanted, ye could get onie shape o a boat made fer ten bob at that day. In nay bit o Perthshire joiners made them.[2]

No doubt some joiners supplied the local people who also enjoyed pearl fishing. Sandy explains the other necessary piece of equipment:

Ye got a can—cut the bottom oot o it, cut a roon gless wae a whitestane an got some caunle wax. Ye dreepit the caunle wax round the gless an it stuck tae yer joug then. Melt in pitch wed hae dae fer its good meltin stuff and melts like oil wi ye. Ye needit a big lang stick an ye pit a split in the end o yer stick. Then we wadit intae the water, lookit doon through yer joug tae see the shells, an then wi yer stick ye dabbit them ontae hit. Ah've seen us hall drove ous spendin a hale day at it—fillin bags wi shells an takin them tae the bankin an openin them. Lots ye never get nothin in, but ye micht open the first wan ye got—it was yer luck wae them. Ah've seen me eleven year auld an gettin them in Tay water.[3]

The travellers found a ready market for their pearls with the Perth jewellers, especially the Cairncross family business as it was then, in St John Street. Local people had them made up into rings for their women folk. An amendment to the Wildlife and Countryside Act made the fishing of mussels for pearls illegal.

As well as making and mending tin ware and pearl fishing, these resourceful people would turn their hand to any kind of work that was available on the farms and in the berryfields. Mechanisation has made their services redundant in these areas. Increased traffic on the roads and the disappearance of many of their traditional camping sites has driven the old style traveller, with his family and all his worldly goods piled on a cart, off the road. They served a useful function in their day and added colour to the rural scene, but modern living has no time for them.

1. R. Leitch, *The book of Sandy Stewart* (Edinburgh 1988), 2–3.
2. Ibid., 41
3. Ibid., 42

A travelling tinsmith at work in the 1920s. [Roger Leitch]

Inns

The travellers in Scotland in the eighteenth century, as well as contending with roads that were often little more than dirt tracks, were fortunate if they came upon a good inn in which to rest at night. R. Haldane observes in *New Ways through the Glen* 'Men and women on the roads, it seemed, must do without, or at least be content with wayside houses not worthy to be called inns, where accommodation was of the roughest and the fare little more than porridge, oatmeal bannocks and illicit whisky.' [1] This view was backed up by Elizabeth Grant of Rothiemurchus who, writing in 1812, noted 'We never see such inns now, no carpets on floors, no cushions on chairs, no curtains on windows,' [2] while Thomas Sommerville recalled that on a journey people used to carry a knife and fork in a case and that glasses were in short supply, a single glass being passed around a large company.

Different travellers, of course, had different expectations and the records they left are subjective but, in the absence of documentary evidence, we have to rely on their tales. There were various types of accommodation, ranging from the disreputable whisky houses through to the change houses and inns proper. What would satisfy a drover would be found inadequate for the travellers from England who ventured north following the building of the turnpike roads.

James Hogg had a very unpleasant experience in a public house between Pitlochry and Killiecrankie when he was involved in a fracas with the other company whose suspicions were aroused when he asked for information about the locality. Dorothy Wordsworth was also glad to see the last of that place. Some miles further north, however, Hogg had a very rewarding stay at Dalnacardoch. Bishop Forbes seemed to have a much happier experience when he ventured on his Episcopal visitation in 1762. At Fortrose he had the best meat with good claret and white wine, followed by fruit after dinner. Mrs Mackinnon's Tavern at Inverness he voted one of the best taverns ever, while at the inn at Dusdale Mrs Innes offered them a choice of green tea, a type of black tea called bohea, tea or coffee at breakfast.

Both the inns at Inver acquired a good reputation, the Ferry inn catering for travellers crossing at the west ferry, while those travelling from Perth through the Bishopric to Strathtay could break their journey and rest their horses at the Inver inn.

Before the Atholls acquired Inver in 1689 the right of ferry was held by John Robertson. The next mention of the boats is in a disposition of 1687 in favour of James Porter, Boat of Inver. The Porter family appear to have had the right of ferry until 1733 when, 'My Lady Duchess sett in tack to Gilbert Weddal the Boats of Invar with two acres of the park of Invar possesst by Robt. Porter for seven years after Whitsun next'. [3] Weddal had to pay £110 Scots for the boats plus £16 and 7 poultry for the land. He also had the 'Boat of Brand' which appears to have plied before the Inver bridge was built about 1740 Weddal did not operate the ferries for long , for in 1740 James Johnston younger produced a tack for nineteen years from 1740 of the three boats of Inver for which he paid £120 Scots and 7 poultry. He also had cottar houses for the servants who were obliged to load and unload His Grace's and his servants' baggage when they used the ferry, free of charge. [4]

Previously, in 1739, Johnstone had acquired possession of the inn as well as the boats, but it is unclear as to whether this refers to Inver Inn or the Ferry Inn. The situation at Inver at that time was, from an examination of the rentals and tacks, very unclear ,with the arrival within a few years

Inver ferry and the Ferry inn by Alexander Naysmith, 1810. [Blair Castle]

of each other of James Johnstone from Dunkeld to take charge of the ferry boats and Charles McGlashan to take charge of the mills.

In the absence of any description of the Ferry inn, we have to rely on a painting by Alexander Naysmith (1758–1840). As he was particularly interested in architectural subjects, we can assume that it is an accurate depiction of the two storeyed building . Miss Murray McGregor, writing in 1861, describes the building thus:

> Following the same track which the ground officer, Sandy Stewart, informed us was the old Bishopric road leading to the ferry, we came to the old Boat House, a two storied [sic] building, quite picturesque, from the luxuriousness of the ivy clustering on the gable next the river ... we went upstairs, rather a broad stair, with a peculiar pattern of flat balustrade, very nearly the same as on the stair of the old inn at Inver. [5]

These descriptions lead to the speculation that the two buildings may be of the same age and have been designed and built by the same person.

The building of the Hermitage and the laying out of the surrounding garden in 1757–8 attracted hordes of visitors to the beauty spot in the ensuing years. James Johnstone, in addition to his duties as ferryman and host at the inn, was put in charge of overseeing the guides and reporting on the

The Hermitage sketched by Lady Emily Murray in 1810. [AA 1512]

state of the gardens. His letters to Sir John Murray, the Duke's nephew who had been responsible for the whole Hermitage project, gives some idea of the variety of visitors passing through Inver at that time. In June 1762 there was good crop of strawberries. Unfortunately, 'the crowd of goats whey people couldn't keep their hands off them'. [6] As a result, a system of issuing cards showing the visitors name was introduced. Mr McGlashan at the inn was also to direct the travellers coming by road from the south to Johnstone for a permit. Visitors were then escorted to the Hermitage under the directions of a guide who ensured that they confined themselves strictly to certain paths. Johnstone reported in August that this had had the desired effect, 'as it kept off the lower class of people from making such repair to it . . . '! [7] Other travellers, such as Lord and Lady Sutherland, Lord Greville and Lord Abercairny were much more welcome, especially if they were to be supplied with refreshments at the inn, or if they were being entertained by the Duke. 'His Grace has given me notice that Him and the Duchess is to supp there soon on cold rost chicken which he says must be got from our house'. [8]

James Johnstone died in 1764 and was succeeded by his son James, whose reign was short for he died in 1770, leaving a string of creditors anxious to recoup their losses from the proceeds of the roup sale. From the inventory of this sale, it is possible to piece together the furnishings of the rooms and come to the conclusion that the various reports that it was a good inn were justifiable.

In the kitchen there was a good supply of cooking utensils ensuring travellers of a hearty meal: a roasting spit, gridiron, skellet pan, frying pan, girdle, pots of brass, copper and iron with the necessary equipment for supporting them over the open fire. A maskin vat and worst stone, tubbs, copper, working vat, barrels bottles and stoups all indicate that ale was brewed on the premises. For those who preferred tea, there were kettles and teapots. Meals were served on tables spread with cloths and supplied with napkins. Broth was supped from pewter trenchers, meat on pewter trenchers or tin plates, with cutlery supplied—no need to carry your own. There were cups, saucers and silver teaspoons for the tea drinkers, stoups for the ale and whisky drinkers—but no glasses!

When they retired for the night, there was for the distinguished guests a bed with curtains, with linen sheets, blankets, bolster and pillows on a feather bed. For the rest there was a chaff bed on a bedstead but there were plenty of blankets. There were also plenty of chairs, chests and even a mirror and a desk. A quantity of lint and spinning wheels indicated that Mrs Johnstone and her daughters kept the house supplied with table and bed linen.

What kind of fare would the traveller be offered? From the kitchen equipment and tableware we can assume that a good meal would be served. As the Johnstone's had a tack of the fishing on the Tay, salmon would be on offer as well as trout from the Braan and the hill lochs in Strathbraan, all in due season. At the weekly market in Dunkeld beef, veal, mutton and pork were traded and the two butchers there were selling beef and mutton at $2^1/_2$d. per pound, pork and veal at 2d. per pound, a goose at a shilling, a duck at 7d. and a hen at 6d., so there was plenty of food available. In addition, the Johnstones had milk and cream from their own cow and they would churn their own butter. There was not much variety of vegetables available but there would be an ample supply of potatoes, turnips and kail, while the garden would yield gooseberries as well as black and red currants.

The staff consisted of three men servants earning from £4 to £5 per year and three maid servants paid less than £2 per year. Presumably that was all found. Johnstone also had the services of his family. John, his second son, followed his father as innkeeper but lasted only a couple of years. James Johnstone's creditors were mostly local wrights, local farmers and merchants in Perth and Dunkeld. One wonders how a thriving inn could get into such financial difficulties. His funeral expenses in 1770 amounted to £8. 14s. 6d. sterling. Thus ended the Johnstone's thirty years reign as boatmen and innkeepers of the Ferry inn.

Andrew Duff succeeded John Johnstone in the Ferry inn in 1774. He must have had a good reputation for in 1783, following the death of James Fisher, he was given the tenancy of Inver inn as well. He seems to have continued to run both inns successfully for the *Old Statistical Account* for Little Dunkeld states, 'There is always a very good inn at Inver'. [9] Indeed, the Duke was so pleased with his performance that his rent of the Inver inn was reduced by £10 as a gratuity as an old servant. Duff died in 1794.

Peter McGillewie succeeded Duff as boatman and ferry keeper while Alexander McGlashan was put in charge of Inver inn along with the mills. Charlie Macintosh has left us a picture of McGillewie who, on hearing a hoolet crying in the middle of the night, threw open his bedroom window and cried out 'Is it the muckle boat or the little boat you're wanting?' [10]

Elizabeth Grant has left us a delightful picture of the inn in 1804:

> On this journey I first remember old Niel Gow being sent for to play us at the inn at Inver—not Dunkeld: that little village we passed through and went on to the ferry at Inver, which we crossed the following morning in a large boat. It was a beautiful ferry, the stream full and deep and dark, the banks overhanging with fine timber trees.... I don't know whether this did not make more impression on me than Niel Gow's delightful violin, though it had so excited me the evening before that my father had taken me a little walk by the river side in the moonlight before I was rational enough to be left to sleep.... As for William, he took all in an easy Ironside way, remarking nothing but the peat reek, which neither he nor I had noticed before. [11]

Great changes were afoot for Inver inn and the ferry. Building of the Dunkeld bridge commenced in 1805 and was completed in March 1809. Niel, before he died in 1807, had composed his last tune 'Dunkeld Bridge'. He must have pondered the great changes taking place around him, with the cutting of the new lade, the proposed new sawmill and soon no more ferry crossings. It would mean a half mile walk for the Inver people to access the new bridge. Elizabeth Grant, writing in 1812, voices the regret which many people must have felt, despite the obvious improvements wrought by the new bridge:

> When next we passed our boundary river the handsome bridge was built over it at
> Dunkeld. The little inn at Inver was done up, a fine hotel where the civilest of landlords
> reigned, close to the bridge received all the travellers; and Niel Gow was dead, the last of
> our bards—no one again will ever play Scotch music as he did. [12]

After the opening of the Dunkeld Bridge there is no reference to Peter McGillewie in the rentals. He just disappears from the scene. The fate of the inn can be traced, however. At first it seems to have lain empty, then gradually adapted to accommodate various tenants. The stable and an out house were converted into dwellings. By 1817 there were five tenants housed in what was now called the old boat house; three of them were widows, setting a policy of housing widows and spinsters who would possibly otherwise have been rendered homeless, for they are frequently described in the rentals as paupers or unable to pay any rent. By 1820 the building was again adapted to accommodate workmen employed by the sawmiller who was responsible for the rent.

The 1830 survey and plan of Inver lists the old boat house occupied by people employed at the saw mills with an adjoining room occupied by Joseph Sim. The cottage housed Charles Connacher, a retired forester, while the stable and byre lay vacant although it was later to house Grizel Farquharson who was removed from the disreputable ale house where she lodged travellers for 4d. a night.

We get a much clearer picture of the building and its occupants from Miss Murray McGregor's account when she and the Duchess Anne visited there in 1861.

Thomas Harris, who had just acquired the tenancy of the sawmill, used the lower part for storage, except for three rooms occupied by John Kennedy, a sawmiller in his employment. The 1861 Census records that Kennedy occupied three rooms, Miss McGregor states two rooms. Upstairs they found:

> To the left in a large room lives Widow Crerar, her abode was very light but possibly as she
> herself said very cold in winter. She is an old woman receiving relief from the parish. In
> the other room we found an aged man dressed in a Sunday coat with brass buttons, it had
> doubtless been made when he held himself more upright for the effect was to draw back
> his shoulders, caused his head which was very neat and small to hang down in a bowed
> shape—he shook hands with us and at once poured forth a torrent of eloquence.... [13]

He told them about his sons, one in Australia, one in New Orleans, one in Gravesend and another in Glasgow. He had been reading from a large book that lay open with his spectacles on it. It was a commentary of the Bible which he read to keep him from wearying. His name was James Arthur and the census record states that he was a retired hand loom weaver:

A low building attached to the boat house we found occupied by Widow Stewart, a little thick set woman with a dark upper lip. She said I think that she had a daughter living with her. 'Her man' she told us was killed about six years ago in a quarry at Birnam, having broken his back....[14]

This was the pattern of occupancy of the boat house, stables and cottage until the early 1900s. Kitty McDonald, the inspiration of Beatrix Potter's character Mrs Tiggy-winkle, occupied a room there from 1891 until she died in 1904. By 1909 there was only one occupant of the building, John McKay, an estate joiner.

The rentals of 1928 state bluntly 'Boat house burned' indicating the final chapter of this once thriving inn which had welcomed generations of weary travellers and latterly provided a final haven for so many single folk. All that remains of it now is a grey stone wall in Jeremy Law's garden.

With the appointment of Mr McGillewie to take charge of the ferry inn, the estate factor set about finding a suitable tenant for the Inver inn. The successful applicant would have to be able to run the corn and lint mills efficiently, have sufficient capital to stock the place and, of course, be of good reputation. Alexander McGlashan, son of Charles, seemed to meet these requirements despite the fact that at times, 'he indulged himself rather too much in drinking with his own companions'.[15] It was hoped that once he had his own house to run he would act differently. His father was able to put up the capital and his brother John was a millwright. A further recommendation was that he had served as a waiter for seven or eight years with Duff at the ferry inn:

> where he was well liked by the travellers and he thereby knows all the families who pass to and fro from the north. He has an advantage the others could not have, besides he knows from that how to keep the house, so that with the assistance of his brother in the mills, I hope he will do.[16]

Alas, McGlashan did not enjoy his tenancy for long, as a note from the factor to the Duke in January 1797 observes, 'McGlashan the innkeeper at Inver has just died—a victim of his own wares'.[17] Mrs McGlashan, Alexander's widow, carried on the inn. Her tenancy was almost as exciting as the former Mrs McGlashan who was caught up in the Jacobite affray.

The hated Militia Act of 1797 sought to raise men as a local defence force because of the fear of a French invasion—a sort of eighteenth century Home Guard. It was bitterly opposed by the population who feared that it would lead to the menfolk being enlisted for service overseas. As a result there were riots in many districts, including Atholl. A rabble rouser by the name of Cameron, nicknamed 'King Cameron', along with one Menzies who operated from Kirkton of Weem, raising rebels from Rannoch through Strathtay to Logierait. The Duke of Atholl alerted the Lord Advocate to the dangers, resulting in a troop of Windsor Foresters being sent from Perth to Weem under Captain Coberg to apprehend the ringleaders. During the night of 13 and 14 September 1797 both men were taken prisoner, immediately being escorted to Perth in a chaise.

Hundreds of Highlanders armed with forks, fowling pieces, pikes and scythes fixed on poles, descended on the troops, leading to a nasty situation which Captain Coberg succeeded in defusing, making speed for Inver, there to rest and feed the horses. It was not long before the mob appeared in sight, obliging the captain to bundle the prisoners into the chaise, saddle the horses and make a bolt for Perth, leaving his men to deal with the mob. In the melee, shots were fired, while some of the crowd pursued the chaise intent while others stayed in Inver boasting of plans to cause future trouble. Cameron and Menzies were held at Perth before being escorted to Edinburgh where Cameron was charged with sedition. Finally, the following January, he was released on bail and promptly absconded, possibly to America. Menzies, along with other rioters, was brought to trial at Perth.

During the night of 23 September another party of militia was despatched to Inver, where the inhabitants were thought to be harbouring trouble makers, including Alexander Stewart who was suspected of firing the gun and a McGregor who was responsible for killing the schoolmaster in Fincastle. The wanted men, however, had earlier made their escape but later all the wanted rebels were captured and convicted at Perth.

Mrs McGlashan, who carried on until 1810, was the last tenant to jointly run both the inn and the mills. When John Crerar became innkeeper extensive repair work was carried out on both the inn and the stables which were re-roofed with slates from the Newtyle quarry, the building also finally being painted. Although Crerar no longer had the tenancy of the mills, he still worked the farm. Even so, the loss of revenue from the mills must have meant a considerable drop in income. There was also a loss of custom from travellers from the north who now used the Dunkeld bridge on their way to Perth, by-passing Inver altogether. Although the inn still remained a focal point for parish business, its heyday had passed and its gradual decline begun.

The building and out houses were deteriorating as Widow Crerar, who succeeded her husband, complained to the factor in 1826, 'I am afraid that my house will fall every night and really my cattle are in danger of being smothered for five of the couples are entirely broke'. [18]

Earlier, in January 1826, Widow Crerar was indirectly involved in a most distressing episode, when witnesses statements were taken at the inn. Who took these, or for what purpose, is not indicated on the documents [19] but they refer to a gruesome incident involving a grave robbery in Little Dunkeld churchyard. Body snatchers had been carrying out their murky activities in Scotland's burial grounds since the beginning of the eighteenth century when the teaching of anatomy was first introduced into the training of medical students. By the end of that century, when the number in the medical faculties was increasing, demand for fresh bodies was outstripping supply. This gave rise to organised grave robbing involving a network ranging from the sexton who dug the grave, the local doctor who knew only too well the likely occupant of the next grave and the carters who supplied the transport, right up to the anatomists in the colleges. These activities gave rise to a wealth of macabre stories circulating around the countryside, causing alarm among the bereaved parishioners who still believed in the resurrection of the body on the day of Judgement.

Our story begins in Inver inn where four cronies sat drinking in Widow Crerar's number two parlour one January night in 1826. James Duff, the weaver, was late in arriving as he had been to the Inchewan distillery to collect draft to feed his cows. There he had been given a good drink so he was 'hearty' before he joined his pals at Inver. Their conversation turned to the death of the Crichton child, Archibald Gibson remarking that the doctors would be interested in the body to investigate the complaint of which the child died. Mention was made of suspicious persons in the district who might be planning to take the body.

James Duff left the inn alone around nine o'clock in a state of such inebriation that his recollection of his movements for the remainder of the night are conveniently vague. He met in with Brodie, the carter, and walked towards Little Dunkeld churchyard where he shouted 'Watch' and heard a gun fired. He met a couple in a cart, the man carrying a gun, stating that had he been sober he would have recognised them. If Brodie was ever suspected, he seemed in the clear as the toll keeper at Dalpowie said his cart was not carrying a heavy load when he passed in the early hours of the morning. Duncan Seaton, an Inver cottar who was the grave digger, was also questioned. All the witnesses were vague and contradictory. We learn more of the nights events in a letter to the factor from William Harris, Middle Inchewan, requesting permission for the parishioners to build a body safety house in the churchyard. [20]

The child's grave was indeed robbed. As was quite usual, or perhaps because they had been disturbed by Duff, the robbers hid the body. It was unfortunately found by a pack of dogs and horribly mutilated. The gruesome discovery prompted the parishioners to open the graves of other recent interments, discovering to their horror that the coffins were empty. Body snatchers were very methodical, taking great care after they removed the body to close the empty coffin, replacing the earth and turf thus leaving no trace of their activities.

A rota of parishioners was drawn up to act as watchers in the churchyard throughout the night. This was possible during the summer but out of the question in the severe winter months. Sufficient money was collected to build a body safety house in the churchyard, all that was required was the consent of the heritors to proceed with the plan. There is no record of whether such permission was ever granted, nor is there any trace of any such structure in the graveyard. Strangely too, there is no report of the gruesome incident in the local press. All that we know of it, apart from letters to the factor, are the confused ramblings of a few Inver topers meeting in number two parlour of Widow Crerar's inn.

To this day, the crack on Niel Gow's gravestone is attributed to gunfire by the body snatchers.

Alexander Fraser, the widow's hosteler and one of the cronies in number two parlour that night, took over the running of the inn for a few years. Before his death in 1830, the 5th Duke's intention was to build a new inn and consequently the building had been allowed to fall into a state of disrepair. Fraser pleaded to the trustees to restore a covered way between the main building and one of the wings so that 'persons sleeping at his inn may cross without exposure to the rain'. [21] His request was refused as the trustees were hoping to find a tenant who would put the building in good order.

William Pullar took on the tenancy in 1841 but after a year he too was complaining:

> I can plainly see that it will be impossible for me to pay the yearly rent of £70 and I am aware that you know of the depressed state of trade and how little is doing in the public house way—and I can assure you that although I have nothing to pay for the house as rent, the taxes and window lights will take all that we can make in the selling of any liquor. [22]

However, he must have been doing a certain amount of trade for the 1841 census shows him employing one hosteler, three female servants and a boy of ten, the brother of one of the servants. The farm attached to the inn was seventeen acres.

The estate, still undecided what to do with the inn, was unwilling to grant a lease to the innkeeper who was, naturally, reluctant to spend any money on repairs to a building which he rented on a year to year basis. In 1851 Thomas Scott was paid £66 by the estate for taking off the roof of the inn, rebuilding the back walls, putting on a new roof, laying floors and sundry other repairs. The 1851 census shows Pullar's son William employed on the farm along with two labourers and a cowherd, while two maids assisted in the inn.

A charming advertisement for Inver Inn about 1861. [HJ]

A report in the *Perthshire Courier* of 23 March 1854 gives a glimpse of the kind of hospitality on offer when Mr William Harris, a well known linen manufacturer in Middle Inchewan, was giving a dinner and presentation in the Old Bridge Hall situated at Inver inn farm. After a sumptuous dinner and toasts, the company were entertained to music supplied by Duncan McKerchar, known as the Athole Paganini, great praise being accorded to Mr Pullar.

In 1861 the Inver inn changed hands for the last time, when it was taken over by Thomas Jackson. He had come from Lancashire to Birnam as a railway contractor whose job it was to supervise the newly opened railway track from Perth to Dunkeld. An ambitious young man, one of his first ventures was to build the villa of Birchwood in 1858 on one of the new feus let by Sir William Stewart of Murthly. Shortly after he had taken over the Inver inn, the Duchess Anne paid him a visit, accompanied by her cousin Miss Murray McGregor, who wrote:

> This afternoon (Monday) Her Grace and I set out in the phaeton with Dr McDonald, to see the improvements proposed by Mr Jackson at the inn at Inver. The new tenant has already freshly papered and painted the house with good effect. He is now erecting a fence round the space in front of the inn and intends having a grass plot and rock work in the centre. The cabbage gardens beyond the stables he wishes to remove and in their stead to have terraced tea gardens leading to the ruins of Neil Gow's house, which he desires to restore. We looked with satisfaction at all these contemplated arrangements. [23]

Alas, these bold plans came to naught. Like too many people involved in the development of the new village of Birnam, Jackson over-reached himself and got into financial difficulties. Birchwood was sold in 1863 and Inver inn was abandoned the same year.

The estate decided to convert the fifteen roomed building into six dwellings, mainly for workers employed at the sawmill. With the stables adjoining, it was the ideal house for Duncan Seaton, the carter, to bring up his family. Apart from the sawmillers, railway workers from the newly constructed Highland line were also housed there. Much to the delight of the youngsters in the village, James Lowe, the retired rector of the Royal School, Dunkeld, was another tenant. He was a keen astronomer who shared his enthusiasm with Charlie Macintosh and his friends by inviting them to view the stars through his telescope.

When the boat house feel into disrepair, widows were housed in the old inn, while part of the building was used as a bothy for estate workers. In 1907 David Keir, the head forester, wrote to the Duke expressing the thanks of the local workmen for the reading room which had been constructed in the left wing of the building. The reading room was taken over by the Girls' Forestry Corps during World War I. They also occupied some of the rooms upstairs. Compared to the Girls' Forestry Corps in the Second World War, who undertook the heavy work of tree felling and had to fend for themselves in Spartan conditions, the female foresters at Inver seemed pampered. They were employed at Ladywell nursery doing light work such as thinning and brushing. Their rooms were cleaned by Mrs Robertson who lived in the nearest cottage.

On Saturday 13 July 1918 some of the young women decided to go for a swim in the River Tay. Unfortunately, they chose a most dangerous spot, the Rock Pool at Inverwood just above the croy. Local people, had they been asked, would have warned them, directing them instead to Pool Dancie on the Braan. One of the girls got into difficulties, the others went to her rescue and all three drowned. Their bodies were recovered by the Newfoundlander foresters working on Craig Vinean. Bill Edwards, a boy at the time, still remembered in old age the flat Atholl estate lorry bearing the three coffins going through a village plunged into gloom.

It is amazing how this old building keeps renewing itself. The right wing was burnt down in the 1960s and rebuilt. The main part, which dates back to at least the seventeenth century when it was occupied by John Robertson of Lude, was renovated in 1995. The stripped walls revealed a stone structure with no liming. The workmen said that it was the oldest building that they had ever worked on. It is to be hoped that it will long continue to give its distinctive character to the village of Inver.

1. A.R.B. Haldane *New ways through the Glens* (Newton Abbot 1973) 178.
2. Elizabeth Grant of Rothiemurchus *Memoires of a Highland lady II* (Edinburgh 1988) 208
3. Atholl Archives 22/16
4. Ibid., 17/58
5. A.A. Bundle 893.
6. Ibid., 49/1/156 It was fashionable for visitors to drink goat whey when they were in the country.
7. Ibid., 49/1/ 210
8. Ibid., 49/1/ 210
9. O.S.A. 1792 p 417
10. Sir Alexander Muir Mackenzie *Tacketies and tyres in Strathbraan* (Perth, 1908)
11. Elizabeth Grant of Rothiemurchus *Memoires of a Highland lady II* (Edinburgh 1988) 44
12. Ibid. Vol. I 206.
13. A.A. Bundle 893
14. Ibid. Bundle 893.
15. A.A. 59/2/86
16. Ibid., 59/2/86
17. Ibid., 59/4/14
18. Ibid., Bundle 1033
19. Ibid., 69/4/382
20. Ibid., 69/4/383
21. Ibid. Bundle 1129
22. Ibid. Bundle 1138
23. Ibid., Bundle 983.

Drink

It is a common misconception that whisky has been the favourite tipple of the Highlander from time immemorial but Colonel David Stewart of Garth avers that ale was once the principal drink among the country people and French wine and brandy among the gentry. [1] Marian McNeill confirms this and quotes what the guidewife of Lochrin produced from a peck of malt:

> Twenty pints o' strong ale
> Twenty pints o' sma',
> Twenty pints o' hinky-pinky (weak beer)
> Twenty pints o' plooman's drinkie,
> Twenty pints o' splitter splatter
> And twenty pints was waur nor watter. [2]

No doubt Margaret Young, the brewster in Inver, had a similar output. When she inherited the brewseat in 1730 it was already well established. It consisted of two acres of land, a house and a yard for which she paid yearly £13. 6s. 8d., six hair of yarn and one pint of honey. For the liberty of brewing she paid £6 Scots and seven poultry. There is no record of what the structure consisted of, but probably it was like most of the brewhouses of the period, a two storey building with each room inside numbered and each utensil used for brewing lettered. This enabled the exciseman, who lived nearby, to check at every stage of the process for tax purposes.

We know from her inventory that she made her own malt. This was usually done in autumn after the harvest as the process required cooler conditions. First the barley was measured and placed in a square wooden coble, possibly lined with stones, over which water was run. As there was no well nearby, it would either be rain water or water drawn from the River Braan close by. The barley was steeped in the coble for a couple of days, after which the water was drawn off and the grain spread out to dry. When it began to germinate it was put on the malting floor and turned regularly with a wooden shovel, for about a fortnight, to increase germination. The grain was then dried in a kiln over a peat fire and stirred at intervals to ensure even heat. The length of drying time determined the eventual colour of the malt, either pale or darker brown. The malt was then sent a short way down the road to the mill, there to be ground and made ready for masking.

The ground malt was put in a vat and boiling water poured over it. It was then covered and left to infuse for two or three hours. The resulting liquor wort was drained off into the copper and mixed with boiling water. At this point more hot water could be run over the mash for a second brewing which produced the weak ale greatly favoured for daily drinking and known as Tuppeny. Hops were not used in Scotland in the first half of the eighteenth century so Margaret Young would flavour the liquor at this stage with broom, heather or honey. After the boiling wort was cooled, yeast was added to start the fermentation process which lasted a few days. The liquor was then drawn off into casks ready for use.

At each stage of the process Margaret had to use her judgement as she was without the benefit of the instruments which today we take for granted. For instance, she had no thermometer and had to test the temperature by seeing how long she could hold her hand in the liquor. She judged that it had come off the boil when the liquid was still enough to give an unbroken reflection. For all that 'she could not wryte' we know from her inventory that she was quite a successful business woman in a position to lend money to neighbours. When she died she left 100 merks for her funeral expenses.

1. D. Stewart of Garth, *Sketches of the Highlanders of Scotland* (Inverness 1885), Vol. I. 237.
2. M. McNeill, *The Scots cellar* (Edinburgh 1956), 4.

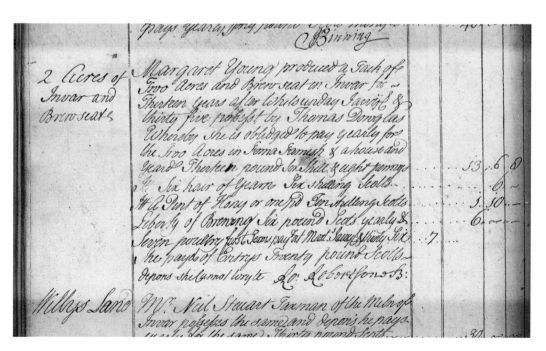

Entry for Margaret Young in 1735 Rental. [Blair Castle]

Exciseman John Anderson

Besides the brewster there were others in Inver who were licensed to sell ale, most importantly James Johnstone who had the ferry inn. Kennedy the fisherman who plied a small ferry at Inverwood, John Gow at the smiddy and Charles McGlashan the inn keeper were also licensed to sell ale and spirits to travellers. The task of keeping an eye on their activities, as well as collecting taxes on soap, salt, candles and malt, fell to John Anderson the exciseman.

His was not a popular calling, since he was distrusted by the community and received little backing from the authorities. Despite this, Robert Burns makes it clear in his letters how patronage was an essential step to achieving a foothold on the ladder. After acceptance, six weeks training in Edinburgh was supposed to be sufficient to fit the aspirant for the task. He was then appointed to a division consisting of a number of parishes, for which he was paid £35 a year. The attraction was that it was a regular income with opportunities for promotion. In addition, the exciseman was entitled to a percentage of the fines and seizures of goods. This did not always amount to much since many of the landlords who sat as magistrates in the Excise Courts were reluctant to fine tenants who were due them rent. Making an inroad into the salary of the exciseman was the rent of his house and yard and the expense of stabling his horse, which was vital to enable him to cover the extensive tract of his division.

After the Malt Tax of 1725 which imposed six pence on every bushel of malt, ale declined in popularity and whisky gradually became the favourite tipple of people. Gaugers now had to turn their attention to the distilleries as well as checking the brewhouses. Owing to the improved agricultural methods of the day, farmers found that they could grow a surplus of barley which they used to produce whisky in their own small stills. It was highly lucrative as the grain residue, called draff, which was left after the whisky was made, could be used as additional animal feed.

An act of 1793 forbad the operation of stills producing less than 500 gallons of whisky except above the Highland line where small stills producing 300 gallons continued to legally function. The dividing line north of Perth was Auchtergaven. This resulted in a thriving illicit trade in the Sma' Glen, Little Glenshee, Amulree and the Little Dunkeld area. The excisemen had an impossible task trying to outwit the wiles of Strathbraan farmers intent on smuggling their liquor to Perth. James Stewart, the Dunkeld poet, celebrated in rhyme the most famous of these encounters, when the Scots Greys were routed by the smugglers at Corriemucklach in the Sma' Glen in 1823. Niel Gow, writing to his son Nathaniel in Edinburgh in 1802 complains, 'As for whisky, the gadgers will not let a drop of it pass our way. They took, last week, three hundred and eighty pints going to Perth down Glenshee, but I will see and have some for you by the time you come to see me'. [1]

So unpopular were excisemen that they were moved on every three years or so. No doubt the authorities did not want them to become too closely integrated into the community. It is therefore surprising to find Mr George Shorthouse, in a memorial to the church and parish of Little Dunkeld, stating in 1825 that he had been a Supervisor of Excise at Dunkeld for fifteen years. His duties took him two or three times a week into Strathbraan, visiting the many licensed maltsters there. He reports that often in desperate cases in the Excise Court, he found the people pretended that they could not take the oath or converse in English, believing that they had in Gaelic some way of evading the oath or satisfying their conscience. He told the justices that, from his own experience of them, he knew that they were quite conversant with English and accordingly they were forced to take the oath and be examined in English, which they were perfectly able to do.

In 1830 the prohibition on small stills was relaxed. The distillery at Inchewan, to which the Inver folk were want to sojourn, finally closed in 1868. Smuggling, which had become a way of life in the area, gradually declined. No longer did the exciseman have to call out the Dragoons to his aid. Peace, of a sort, reigned between tippler and gauger.

Many myths have grown around Niel Gow, portraying him as someone in a constant state of inebriation. His biographer, Joseph McGregor, puts us in the picture when he writes:

> There are few professions where persons are more exposed or tempted to habits of indulgence in liquor than those whose calling is to minister music to the midnight and morning revels. The fatigue of playing for hours in crowded, heated rooms—at those times, too, which are usually devoted to sleep—requires stimulants; and not a few have fallen victims to habits acquired in such situations. But of those exposed to these temptations, as much as any man ever was, Niel Gow was essentially sober and temperate. He never indulged in unmixed spirits, and when at home without company, seldom took any drink but water. [2]

As the picture of Niel sitting at home with Margaret, drinking water, strikes us as a bit fanciful, let us find out what else Niel drank. His sons kept him well supplied, John sending him porter from London and Nathanial, according to McGregor, regularly sent him shrub—a cordial with citrus juice mixed with spirit. When Lord Melville, visiting the cottage one day, was pressed to take some shrub, hesitated, Niel urged, 'Ye maun tak it out, my Lord, it's very good and came frae my son Nathaniel— I ken ye're treasurer o' the navy, but gin ye were treasurer o' the universe, ye maun leave a drap'. [3]

A popular and nutritious drink at that time was, and still is with some to the present day, buttermilk or 'soor deuk' as it was commonly known, as was whey—a by product of cheese making. By the mid eighteenth century tea drinking had become popular for those that could afford it. It is doubtful if it was much indulged in the cottages of Inver but it was certainly served to tourists in the ferry inn.

The Inver men were wont to foregather in the village inn for their mid morning dram. One of the family of McDonald, wright, went each day for his gill. Before tasting it, he reverently took off his bonnet and asked for a blessing. Duke John, on hearing this, was so impressed that he ordered that McDonald was to be served a dram a day for as long as he lived.

By the nineteenth century the clergy, especially those of the Free Church, had become so alarmed at the habits of drunkenness that the Temperance movement was started and grew rapidly throughout Scotland. James Macintosh, brother of Charles, had a flute band and a string band. He believed, along with other musicians, that in order to have enough stamina to play all night at a ball, a dram was an essential. One night he decided to do without and, to his amazement, next day instead of being fagged out he was full of vigour. He determined that in future he would drink no spirits while playing. He became an active member of the Good Templar movement and brother Charles became superintendent of the Band of Hope. Thus the Temperance movement, with its slogan 'The strong man's drink is water' came to Inver. One wonders what old Niel would have made of it.

Perhaps because of the strength of the total abstinence movement, a lemonade factory flourished in Dunkeld under the ownership of the Cuthbert family. Soft drinks such as lemonade, ginger beer and orange squashes were popular, although fortified wines were regularly advertised and consumed, in secret no doubt. Since the 1950s when holidays abroad became de rigeur, people have acquired a taste for wines. The Marshall Plan brought us Coca Cola from America and sadly now youngsters are knocking back Buckfast and cider the way their predecessors drank lemonade.

If you want to go out for a drink in Inver nowadays, you must go to either Birnam or Dunkeld. There is now no one in the village licensed to sell ales and spirits. But Erica Lyon keeps digging up old bottles in Niel's garden.

1. N.L.S. MS 590 No. 1600–1
2. J. McGregor, *Memoir of Niel Gow* (Edinburgh 1837) 2.
3. Ibid. 2.

An old Highland whisky smuggler with a pot still.

Education and schools

Although Inver was the most important village in the parish of Little Dunkeld, neither the parish school nor the parish church were ever located there. These two focal points of any community were always sited in the almost negligible village of Little Dunkeld. Successive schools stood somewhere between the mouth of the Braan and the vicinity of the Little Dunkeld manse.

The young Niel Gow, when he was seven years old, would set off therefore to walk barefoot the half mile or so from Ladywell to Little Dunkeld parish school, carrying with him a peat to replenish the fire which heated the hovel of a classroom. His teacher was most probably John McNaughton, appointed there in 1729, who three years previously had been interviewed by Dunkeld presbytery as to his fitness to teach. They 'found that he is capable to read Inglish and that he gave an agreeable account of his knowledge of the principles of Religion, that he writeth a tolerable good hand and that he knows and practiceth the Common Rule of vulgar arithmetic. . . .' [1] John McNaughton admitted that he could not sing, so it was unlikely he would do much to advance the young lad's undoubted musical talent.

Niel's education would have been confined to the winter months when his parents would pay a modest fee for each quarter to have their sons schooled in the elements of reading, writing and arithmetic, until they were twelve years old or so. However adverse the conditions in which he was taught by a schoolmaster of limited ability, Niel developed into an adult with a shrewd business sense, capably of writing a decent letter. When released from the confines of the classroom, Niel was free to pick out on his beloved kit fiddle the tunes that he heard his mother sing or whistled by packman, drovers and sundry travellers who passed through the village. In the summer months he could thus entertain his brothers and neighbours as they climbed up by the Inchewan Burn to Birnam Hill to cut peats and divots, or to herd the cattle grazing around Inver.

When the time came for his own children to receive their schooling, William, John and Andrew were taught by John Irvine and John Robertson. All that has been said about Niel's education would apply to his sons, although, judging by the way these two teachers kept the parish registers, their instruction would have been of a higher standard. All three sons did well as professional musicians, John possessing in addition an excellent business sense.

The remaining Gow children, Margaret, Grizel and Nathaniel, were taught by Thomas Foggo, who started teaching at Little Dunkeld in 1766. A year later a new school was built at, 'Braan mouth within sight of the walks'. [2] Costing the princely sum of £16. 13s. 5d. cheap even for those days, it must have been an improvement on what had gone before. Foggo's salary was a meagre £5. 11s. 1$^{1}/_{2}$d. per annum, supplemented by the fees paid quarterly for each pupil, 7s. 6d. for reading, 2s. for writing and 2s. 6d. for arithmetic. His pupils were also drilled in Catechism. The teaching, though basic, must have been thorough, as shown by Nathaniel's letter. Later in life, he became one of the most prosperous music publishers and performers in Scotland.

There was no schoolhouse provided, so Foggo commuted daily across the small mid ferry passenger boat to his home in Dunkeld. Like his predecessors, he also kept the parish register and this brought him into conflict with the Little Dunkeld inhabitants. The Militia Act of 1797 obliged him to collect the names of all the young men in the parish between the ages of nineteen and twenty three who were liable for military service. The parents of the young men were so enraged at the thought of their sons being called up that they crossed over to Dunkeld, forced their way into the terrified Foggo's house and seized both the hated list and the parish records. Those dating earlier that 1755 were never recovered, a cause of much frustration to today's genealogists and local historians.

Thomas Foggo retired in 1804 on an annual pension of 200 merks, the longest serving schoolmaster of Little Dunkeld. He had served the community well, but had outlived his efficiency, bequeathing to his successor a run down building and the task of bringing the scholars up to standard again. That man was William McAra, who was no doubt gratified at being promoted from a private school in Tulliebardine to parish schoolmaster in Little Dunkeld. He was engaged to teach reading, writing, arithmetic, book-keeping, hand sewing and Christian knowledge. For an extra fee of 5s. per quarter, pupils could be taught Latin.

McAra was dismayed to find the school building in such a ruinous state and that there was no schoolhouse provided. As his protests to the heritors went unheeded, the parents took up the cudgel on his behalf. In the short time he had been there, they were delighted with their children's progress and they did not want to loose him. In February 1806 they wrote to the Duke of Atholl, one of their heritors, asking for his help:

> The schoolhouse is a perfect hutt or hovel, no way calculated to contain the number of children who daily attend. That number just now exceeds sixty—and when training in the way of writing and arithmetic commences the infants who have only their catechism are obliged to retire. . . . [3]

—to where, one wonders. A new building was provided in 1807.

McAra, in addition to his duties as session clerk, sold Bibles in both English and Gaelic for the Bible Society. He had no Gaelic himself, which was no disadvantage as his pupils came from the Inchewans, Little Dunkeld and Inver, which were all non-Gaelic communities unlike Strathbraan and Bishopric areas where the schoolmasters had to grapple with the problem of teaching in English pupils who knew only Gaelic.

Attendance was not compulsory at that time, many pupils withdrawing in the summer months to help their parents to harvest their acre of land, herding, peat cutting and oak barking. It was usual for children to start schooling at six or seven and to continue for as long as it suited the parents to keep them there. Charlie Macintosh started school at six years, left at twelve, resuming his education two years later at the Royal School of Dunkeld, which he attended for two winters. Miss Marion Wallace informed me that her mother attended Little Dunkeld school until the age of fourteen, when she left to work in Edinburgh. She didn't like the work and returned to school and remained there until the age of seventeen. There was much greater flexibility in the nineteenth century than today.

Yet another school was built in 1822, in close proximity to the old one. An attractive building, it was bought by Dr Culbard in 1872 when the parish school moved to Birnam. Since then the old school has been occupied by successive doctors and now houses the Health Centre for the area.

Peter Lowe wrote from Inver to his son John in America in 1829 telling him that his old schoolmaster, William McAra, had died of an apoplexy in February. His place was to be filled by John Gow and it was hoped that he would be a more popular teacher than preacher.

Formerly Little Dunkeld School, this building is now the doctors' surgery. [HJ]

It was during John Gow's reign as schoolmaster that the Disruption in the Church of Scotland took place in 1843. Many members of Little Dunkeld parish church left to form their own Free Church congregation. They built their own school, a simple wooden structure at what was then known as Wester Inchewan but is now Birnam. The site was by the Inchewan Burn, near what is now the Beatrix Potter garden. It's first headmaster was Mr Sutherland and one of his first pupils was Charlie McIntosh, who now had to trudge the extra half mile from Inver. A report in the *Perthshire Courier* for 5 November 1845 records the school being visited by various benefactors including Mr Fox Maule, Birnam Lodge and Dr Smytten, Birnam Cottage. 'The children were examined for six hours, in every department. Several advanced Latin scholars were absent due to indisposition....'[4] Who could blame them!

The Free Church erected a stone built building at Torwood in 1853 on land acquired from Sir George Stewart of Murthly. This school continued until the Education Act of 1872 did away with the denominational schools. Meantime, John Gow continued teaching in the depleted parish school until he retired in 1861.

The onerous task of moving the parish school from Little Dunkeld to Torwood fell to James Milne, who succeeded John Gow in 1861. The Education Act of 1872 put the school under the jurisdiction of the Scotch Education Department, although they were over-seen at parish level by the local school board on which were represented the ministers of the various churches in the area. Little Dunkeld had two school buildings to choose from, neither of which were adequate.

With the rise in population in Birnam and the school intake extending east of Birnam as far as the Byres of Murthly, Torwood was the sensible site for the new school, although it meant a longer walk for the Inver pupils. While negotiations between the Free Church and the new school board continued, Mr Milne was left to cope with an increased number of pupils in a very inadequate building. Some pupils were taught in his parlour, others in Little Dunkeld church. If the church was required during the week, the scholars were given a holiday!

The school staff at this time was a family affair, with Mr Milne being assisted by his wife and daughter Laura, who was pupil teacher. Under this system, senior pupils helped the schoolmaster with certain lessons, giving them teaching experience, while they themselves received advanced tuition to prepare them for entry into teacher training college. Between them, the Milne family taught 170 pupils at this time. The Inspector's report for April 1875 states, 'Under great disadvantage from want of room, the school has been taught during the year by Mr and Mrs Milne with the utmost fidelity and assiduity. . . . After much delay work has begun on the new school'. [5]

The entry in the school log book, Tuesday 26 October 1875, states 'Entered the New Building Tuesday 26th. The scholars received a half holiday on Monday in consequence of the furniture being moved from the old to the new premises.' The following April, the Inspector reported that the new premises were generally excellent. But Torwood school from the beginning had drainage problems which resulted in a number of serious outbreaks of scarlet fever, diphtheria and measles during the first twenty five years.

The school session started in September and finished in July, with a few holidays during the winter months. There was school as usual on Christmas day, but a few days break at New Year coincided with Hansel Monday which was the principal tradesman's holiday, when there was great jollification. A day off was customary on Thursday before church communion, known as Fast Day. In the spring a few days break was given at Easter and the Queen's birthday in May was also a holiday. During the winter months, the scholars had a short break in the middle of the day when they ate the 'pieces' they had brought with them. The school could thus be dismissed at 2.20 to enable the children to walk home safely before dark.

In addition to the three 'R's', senior pupils were given the option of Latin Rudiments, Elements of French using Hall's French Course, Animal Physiology, Mathematics and Singing, for which the master received extra remuneration. Part of his salary was also made up with the pupils quarterly fees. These were abolished in 1890.

Mr Milne, a graduate of Aberdeen University, retired in 1882 after a life-time of dedicated teaching. He received a pension of £95 per annum, which he lived to enjoy until he died in 1895. John Wallace was the new headmaster who integrated into the life of the community, acting for some time as secretary of the newly formed Birnam Institute and leading the praise as precentor in Dunkeld Cathedral. Beatrix Potter, a visiting member of the congregation, describes him thus, 'Perched just below (the pulpit) is the Precentor—a fine big man with a bullet heady, chubby red face, retreussie nose and a voice like a bull. He is the Birnam schoolmaster'. [6]

Certainly, throughout his reign at Birnam, whatever his other shortcomings, Inspectors always commented favourably on the children's singing.

At this time, ladies living in idleness in the newly built villas of Birnam with a host of servants to tend them, to relieve the boredom of the day would descend upon the school to watch the class work in progress. Mr Wallace's log book is full of reference to these visits, which no other master seems to have encouraged.

11 July 1882   Miss McLagan and Miss Buchan called and spent some time in school while lessons were given. Both were much interested.

18 Feb. 1887   Today the Misses Gibson spent two hours hearing the usual work going on.

29 April 1887   On Wednesday Rev. M. Browlie Glasgow called and on the same day Miss Gibson paid a long visit.

There is no record of what the teachers thought!

24 July 1886   During the week Mrs and Miss Cunningham, Miss Gibson and the Rev. Gibson from Canada, Prince and Princess Salin-Salin (Germany). The latter has given 10/- [ten shillings] for additional prizes on 6th. August.

Perhaps it was the expectation of prizes that encouraged Mr Wallace to permit these intrusions. There were other visits, however, to which he was obliged to acquiesce. Members of the School Board came unannounced to inspect the register, the most frequent of whom were the clergy of the various churches, Parish, Free and Presbyterian.

18 March 1883   2.30. Visited the school. Examined and signed registers and found the classes in each department diligently engaged in their studies. Andrew Keay (member).

10 June 1891   Visited the school this afternoon: found all in excellent working order; some Analysis and some Euclid done by children during visit—both very well done. Attendance fair: atmosphere of school very good. John McAinsh, member .

On the last day of summer term the pupils were examined in religious Knowledge by the local clergy.

22 July 1892   Religious Knowledge Examination held today from 11a.m.–1.30p.m. The Rev. J.S. Mackenzie, Little Dunkeld, and I examined along with the teachers; the results of the examination were very satisfactory; prizes from Lady Stewart and Mrs Logan were distributed. Examined registers and found them neatly kept. John McAinsh, Member.

By 1893 Mr Wallace was obviously bored with the work and contemplating a move. He began to let standards slip.

10 Oct. 1893   Visited the school at 11.50a.m., found work going satisfactorily in Infants department, but no entry has been made in the Log Book or any register marked in Mr Wallace's department since re-opening school. J. Stewart M.B.

Mr Wallace departed the following January and on 5 March Mr John Purdie, the new headmaster, took up duty. The Inspector's report the next month sums up the situation

20 April 1894   The work of Miss Penney's department, Infants Standards I and II, is all very well done and she teaches sewing in all classes thoroughly as well. The late

master has left the Senior Department in a very unsatisfactory state. There is little of the work either oral or written that is well done, and most of it is very bad. His successor, however, comes very well recommended, seems active and energetic and may be expected to bring the school into something like its old form. J.A. Harris, Clerk.

And Mr Purdie, in the following decade, did just that, as his former pupils happily still living can testify. He was engaged at a salary of £150 per annum and, in addition, the school board undertook to build a schoolhouse for him, a handsome villa on the newly developed Perth Road, at a cost of £650. Mr Purdie proved to be the new broom that the school needed. Vulgar fractions, bills of parcels, reduction of money and long division were drummed into the children. Miss Marion Wallace recalls that when exasperation overcame him, instead of counting to ten, he went outside and chalked 'ASSES HALL' in large letters on the door.

The youngsters physical needs were also catered for. Mr McLeish of the School Board reported on 10 December 1894, 'Visited school. Examined registers. Soup is being supplied to the children at mid-day. From practical experience I am satisfied the soup is being properly cooked. The children are taking advantage of the warm dinner.' It was a boon to children such as Peg Edwards who had to walk from Inver. She recalls the delight if she discovered a bone with a bit of meat in her helping. Local farmers were generous in donations of vegetables, while butchers gave bones for the stock.

The curriculum was expanding in other directions. A concert given by the children in the Birnam Institute raised money for school music. Military drill was introduced for the boys and the harmonium was repaired to supply an accompaniment.

Flooding at Torwood School—summer 1912. Drains had long been a problem in the Torwood area and a severe summer storm resulted in flooding. [HJ]

An increase in the school roll necessitated an extra class room, plus an extra teacher. A new gallery was erected in another room which was equipped with dual and triple desks complete with slate racks and ink wells. Winter holidays now commenced at Christmas Day and extended into the beginning of January. But all this encouraging activity came to a halt when the saddest event in the school's history occurred in 1902.

The drains of the school had always been unsatisfactory, protests to George Mackay, the Chief District Sanitary Inspector going unheeded. Parents, alarmed at the state of the sewer in front of the school, kept their children at home. Mr Mackenzie, the minister visiting the school on 4 February 1902, wrote in the Log Book:

> ... as there have now been five deaths of scholars with diphtheria in the last year or thereby—one of them being buried this day—a strong girl of about twelve years—and there are others ill in hospital, or newly discharged at home: as a manager of the school, I regard the case as one of extreme urgency demanding immediate action, and I refuse to take even a day's responsibility for the lives of the children until this sewer and its gratings are reported upon and authoritatively declared to be safe: and I hereby close the school and request the clerk of the School Board to send a copy of this entry in the school Log Book to the Chief District Sanitary Inspector in Perth, to the Local Government Board, and the Department, for all action in the circumstances of the case.

The Inspector's report of May 1902 contained the following excerpt, 'For fifteen months past the school has been conducted under conditions the most adverse and distressing that I have ever encountered. . . . During the re-construction of the drainage . . . the school met in temporary premises.'

These premises were the hall and committee room of the Birnam Institute who gave the use to the scholars for one month, but would not sanction another four weeks as the members, to their shame, complained of the noise of the children. In all, there were fifteen cases of diphtheria, six fatal, including Mr Purdie's son Willie, who died on the 5 March and lies buried in Little Dunkeld churchyard.

The annual report for 1902 concluded, ' . . . I desire to record my opinion of the courage and fidelity with which the school has been carried on through a period of general and private calamity'. Despite this testimony, some Inver parents now chose to send their five year olds to start their schooling at the Royal School Dunkeld, despite the longer walk this entailed for little children. From then on there was a steady trickle of Inver youngsters making their way to the Dunkeld school but they were mostly the children of workers newly arrived in the village.

It was remarked on in the Inspector's report that the pupil's Nature Study was particularly good. This was due, in no small measure, to the visits of Charlie Macintosh, the Perthshire Naturalist. He was, of course, well known to the Inver children as their friendly neighbour 'Tosh'.

His kindly bearded face on top of his long thin frame would appear at the classroom door, his fishing basket in hand completing the picture, ready to take the children on an expedition to Birnam Glen, down to the River Tay or even as far afield as the Hermitage. On these outings they would learn to recognise the different songs of the birds in spring, the names of the wild flowers, the characteristics of the trees on the thickly wooded banks. In autumn they would be introduced to the rare species of fungi which abound in these woods, as well as the lichens and mosses growing on the trunks and walls. Prizes were given to encourage the children to write about these walks and when Charlie died in 1922 a Natural History prize in his name was awarded to Perthshire children who wrote the best essays on Nature Study. It is still in existence and their efforts judged by the Keeper of Natural History at Perth Museum.

During the first part of the twentieth century the school observed various national occasions. In May 1900 a holiday was given in honour of the Relief of Mafeking, one of the gravest incidents in the South African War, where a number of local lads were fighting. The 11 May Mr and Miss Fothringham of Murthly Castle inaugurated the flag staff which he had presented to the school. The pupils were instructed in the constituent parts of the Union Jack before it was hoisted in the name of Queen Victoria and in celebration of the British Empire. No doubt they were also taught the significance of pink on the maps on the school walls. The children were then given a holiday, the first Empire Day, which was to be celebrated for many years to come. Of more significance to Scottish children, on the five hundredth anniversary of the Battle of Bannockburn, on 1 July 1914 they assembled round the flagstaff, hoisted the flag, the Saltire one hopes, and sang 'Scots Wha Hae'.

Strangely, no mention is made of World War I in the log book. Work went on normally throughout those years, although some pupils lost their fathers and brothers in the conflict. But Peg Edwards, Inver, one of those whose father was killed, recalls Mr Purdie standing in tears at the first Armistice service. His son Peter had been killed in action.

Entry in log book 1 April 1920:

John Purdie, headmaster, finishes work at the school this day having been appointed Headmaster at Auchterarder Public school after 26 years service at Birnam School as its headmaster. On Friday, he was the recipient of a gold watch from the community and a gold Albert from staff and pupils as a parting gift.

He was one of that dedicated breed of dominie who earned for Scottish education a reputation for sound teaching. There are those still living in the area who are grateful for the schooling they received from him.

Teachers at Torwood School about 1928.
Left to right: *Mr Lunan, headmaster;*
Miss May Gibb, infants;
Miss Stewart, lower primary and
Miss Ramsay, primary and
Domestic Science.

[HJ]

Mr Charles Lunan M.A., who succeeded Mr Purdie, was destined to be the last headmaster of Birnam School.

In the 1920s there was a very different procession of visitors from those in Mr Wallace's day. The school doctor, the school dentist, the school nurse, all looked after the welfare of the children, a necessity as infectious illnesses continued to take their toll on pupils. Nurse Martin examined the children for 'cleanliness of body and clothes' to detect any signs of scabies or impetigo. Purple blotches of Gentian Violet were the tale signs of those affected. Sandy Stewart, a traveller's bairn attending the school at the time, gave this description of the ordeal to Roger Leitch:

> When we were intae Birnam, as lang as yer claes wir clean on the inside, they wirna particular. Ther usetae be a nurse went aa ower yer heid. The nurse was ginger heidit an she bud intae Dunkel. Then ther wes mair came frae Perth an they examined every skull near. Ye wer taen intae a room an aa yer heid wes lookit; yer claes wis lookit.... That's the wey they got ye, an no only me but the rest o the bairns that bud in the toon. They lookit ower every yin that was there. [7]

Mrs Robertson, Murthly, formerly Miss Gibb, was Sandy's teacher at Birnam. In conversation with Roger Leitch she has left a description of the lay out of the school at that time. She came to Birnam to teach the infants, in place of Miss Menzies who left for a post in Breadalbane Academy. There were four teachers, each with a room, Miss Gibb herself in the big room with the infant classes, Miss Stewart in a smaller room for the juniors, Miss Ramsay in charge of the important qualifying class and Mr Lunan the headmaster teaching the supplementary section.

There were no visiting teachers except Mr Matheson who came from Perth to teach Physical Education, that is, when he succeeded in making the journey to Birnam. He usually travelled by motor bike but it frequently broke down or the weather was too bad. When he acquired a car, it too broke down and he didn't seem to be able to get to Perth station on time for a train. Class teachers were expected to take sewing and knitting, art and music.

Music was no problem as Mr Lunan was a skilled choir master, as was Miss Menzies. The Perthshire Music Competitive Festival was inaugurated in 1921 and Mr Lunan entered his pupils for the rural choirs class. Far from being overwhelmed by the experience of singing in the large City Halls in Perth, the Birnam pupils took first place. To their delight, on their arrival back at the station they were met by a piper who piped them in triumph back to the school. In subsequent years they continued to acquit themselves well, keeping up the high standard of singing which had prevailed at the school for decades.

Singing in school at that time was mostly taught by the tonic sol-fa system which, although limited in its usefulness for modern music, made for great accuracy, good intonation and aural perception. Each class room had a Curwen modulator hanging on the wall by which the children were drilled as thoroughly as they were in their multiplication tables. The living proof of the excellence of the system is in Mrs Malloch, nee Edwards, an Inver pupil under Mr Lunan, who at the age of ninety still sang sweetly in the soprano section of Dunkeld Cathedral choir.

The other work of the school did not suffer as a result of the time spent on music, if anything it gained, as the qualifying results show. Those passing the exam with a high enough mark and sit the bursary examination had the opportunity to continue their education at Perth Academy. But this meant a punishing day for the Inver children, who had the long walk to Birnam station to board the

The Torwood School Choir which won first prize in the
Rural School Choirs' competition at the Perthshire Musical Festival, 1921.
Included in the above, back row: *Marion Wallace; J. White; Violet Kay.*
2nd back row: *W. Sinclair; Margaret Sinclair; Cathy Cramb; Netta Wallace.*
3rd back row: *D. Sinton; ? Williamson; E. Morgan; G. Saunders; Etta Stewart; Dorothy Hardie;*
G. Thomson; Susan Bruce; Cath McInnes; Flo Macdonald; J. Sim; A. Dunbar; Peg Edwards.
Front row: *Mr Lunan (headmaster); Min Keir; M. McNicol; Dinah Balfor; ? McDiarmid.* [Mrs Malloch]

train for Perth, with a further long walk from Perth railway station to the building in Rose Terrace. For some, this was too great a strain on their young constitutions. School buses, indeed a bus service, were in the future.

In 1918 the old School Boards were done away with and County Education Authorities set up in their place. The Perthshire authority in 1926 decided to build a new school to serve the needs of both the Little Dunkeld children and those of the Royal School Dunkeld. A new site near Little Dunkeld church was offered by the Duke of Atholl, building went ahead and the present school was opened by the Duchess of Atholl on 19 April 1930. The Inver children's walk to school was now shorter, indeed very much as it had been in earlier times. At first, the new school had a junior secondary department as well as a primary one, but in 1968/9 with the introduction of the comprehensive system, since when the school has catered for primary pupils only, secondary education being provided either at Breadalbane Academy in Aberfeldy or at Perth.

The closing of Birnam was an emotional occasion for staff and pupils alike. Miss Gibb and Miss Stewart joined the staff under Mr Crombie at the new school of Dunkeld-Birnam Royal School. Miss Ramsay was transferred to Pitlochry and Mr Lunan was appointed headmaster at Craigie school in Perth. He was held in great affection by the pupils and with respect by the staff and the community, carrying on to the last day the fine tradition of devoted teaching, in often unbelievably difficult circumstances, which was given by successive headmasters over a period of some two hundred years at Little Dunkeld.

On 28 April 1930 the management committee presided over the presentation ceremony in the new school. Representatives of the Education Committee, the parents, the Birnam Institute, the W.R.I., the Perthshire Rural Library Scheme and the Dunkeld and Birnam Golf Club, along with Mr John Purdie, attended. After the presentation and the speeches, the meeting closed with the singing of the fourth verse of the second Paraphrase, a prayer which had been sung every afternoon during the long history of the school.

Final entry in the Birnam School log book:

April 29th.   At the opening function of the Dunkeld-Birnam Royal School a combined choir of children from the two schools sang four songs, when Miss Begg, Infant Mistress Dunkeld accompanied and Mr Lunan conducted the singing. [8]

1. S.R.O. CH2/106/5
2. Ibid., CH2/106/8
3. A.A. 48/7/33
4. *Perthshire Courier* 5 November 1845
5. Torwood School Log Book 1875.
6. L. Linder, *The Journal of Beatrix Potter 1881–1897* (London 1989) 266
7. R Leitch, *The book of Sandy Stewart* (Edinburgh 1988) 16.
8. Birnam School Log Book 1930.

Birnam Hostel of the Scottish Youths Hostel Association

Following the closure the school at Torwood, the building was used as a Youth Hostel for a number of years before being demolished when the present A9 road was built to bypass Dunkeld. [HJ]

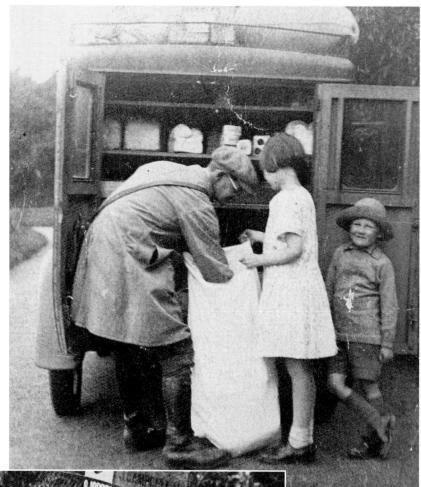

Fresh bread was just one of the many items which conveniently arrived in Inver, while the news and gossip which the van drivers brought was especially welcome to housewives living in the more remote areas of Highland Perthshire.

[HJ]

Women's Education and Employment

It is difficult to assess the standard of education of the Inver women in the eighteenth century since they were seldom asked to sign petitions or put their name to deeds. At that time, and indeed well into the nineteenth century, women's chief role was considered to be marriage, the bearing of children and thereafter the rearing of those children and providing her husband with such domestic comfort as they could afford. In these circumstances girls were expected to sew, wash clothes and spin. The latter accomplishment not only provided the family with napiery and under clothes but was important in earning the money to pay the rent.

Girls could learn these skills from their mother but in 1733, in an attempt to raise the standard of spinning in the area, the Board of Trustees paid for a spinning mistress at £10 a year to teach the girls in Dunkeld. Probably, if they so wished, Inver lasses would be eligible for tuition there. Later, at the beginning of the nineteenth century, a Mrs Archer had a sewing school in Inver, followed by an Infant school run by Mrs Farquharson. However, if the girls wished to learn to read and write, there was the parish school of Little Dunkeld three quarters of a mile along the bank of the Tay or the little school at Torrivall about a mile up the old drove road to Amulree, near Rumbling Bridge.

Whereas it is fortunate that there are letters from Inver men dating from the late eighteenth century and early nineteenth century in the Atholl Archives, there appear to be no letters written by women. On the many testaments and various lists of petitions of that period, the names of only three women appear. Margaret Young, the brewster, of whom it was stated she could not write, Widow Gow, who signed with a bold hand and Margaret Macdonald, Niel Gow's daughter. She must have been a competent, literate woman for she was entrusted to deal with her father's considerable estate when he died in 1807, although she had two brothers more capable of doing so. They appear to have been content to leave it to their sister. Margaret would have been a pupil of Thomas Foggo as would widow Gow. Ability to sign ones name was not necessarily evidence of literacy, but the parents of Inver and Strathbraan showed considerable concern that their children could speak and write English and above all read the Bible. Charles McIntosh observes that during the Crimean war the girls of the village came to his mother asking her to write letters to their men folk in the conflict. This implies that although they could no doubt read, they had not enough confidence or ability to write a letter, even to a dear one! This kind of limited education fitted the girls for employment in domestic service, until they married. If they remained spinsters their fate was to be kept at home to look after ageing parents and, when they died, to perform the same service for any unmarried brothers.

In the 1831 Atholl estates census of Inver the employed women listed are Grizel Farquharson who kept a disreputable lodging house and Elizabeth Borrie, grocer. In the 1841 census only Janet Low, midwife and the above named Elizabeth Borrie are mentioned while in 1851 Mrs Farquhurson is listed as formerly Infant School teacher and Helen Scott is described as a domestic servant and a sick nurse. It is possible that she acted as a midwife. All the above women were widows and all were described as paupers. By 1861, however, in addition to the usual female servants and the redoubtable Elizabeth Borrie, there are listed three dressmakers and three laundresses, indicating that women could now afford these luxuries. The rise of the village of Birnam and the increased tourist trade as a result of the building of the railway also created a demand for services.

In 1861 Duchess Anne, accompanied by her companion, Miss Murray McGregor, visited every house in Inver and their remarks leave us a glimpse of life inside the cottages. One of the people on whom they called was Elizabeth Borrie. Born in Logierait in 1788, she was the daughter of Alexander Campbell, a farmer. She married Donald Borrie who was a member of one of the oldest families in Little Dunkeld parish. He was a carpenter to trade but also set up as a merchant, selling groceries from his cottage in Inver. When he died in 1830, leaving her with a young family, she carried on the business. She did not have an easy start. In 1830 Inver was undergoing a period of reconstruction as part of the development of the sawmilling business. Her husband died in April and in May her house was pulled down and she was temporarily accommodated, along with her neighbour Peter Low, in one of the new cottages being built. It was not a happy arrangement. Peter Low, writing on her behalf to the Duke of Atholl, drew attention to the difficulties:

> ... the poor Widow's groceries ... being kept so near the fire, that it takes away almost all her profit and the unhealthy smell that the soap, sugar, treacle and oil produces on account of the heat, she being obliged to keep these articles within little more than a few feet of the fire—hurts both her health and ours. [1]

Fortunately, both families were soon accommodated in two of the four substantial slated cottages which still stand on the left hand side of the road as you approach the village. There she thrived, later adding a Post Office to her business, until she died in 1864. When Duchess Anne visited her in 1861 she found her paralysed on the right side with a stroke but able to talk and being looked after by her daughter Catherine. Despite her infirmity, Her Grace describes her as a remarkably handsome old woman.

When she died her son Donald carried on the business, now occupying two of the cottages. He also opened a grocery shop in Birnam. Later in the nineteenth century the cottage was occupied by the McDougal family. Their daughter Maud, although styled as a music teacher in the 1891 census, sold soft drinks and biscuits to passing travellers. There was no need for a village grocer in Inver by that time as vans from both Dunkeld and Birnam drew up at the cottage doors to supply the housewives with all their needs. Beatrix Potter in her journal makes numerous references to McDougal whom her father employed when they visited Birnam in 1892.

1. Atholl Archives 69/6/451

The Domestic Scene

Inver women in the eighteenth century were fully engaged with the home front and, in general, did not seek work outside the home. Apart from the usual domestic chores of cooking and cleaning, milking and churning, their main task was spinning in order to earn money to pay the rent. This was seasonal work, starting in the autumn when the dressing of the flax had been completed.

Their supplies mostly came from crops grown around Inver as well as from Strathbraan and the Bishopric, although Charlie Macintosh states [1] that his grandmother obtained her flax from Blair Atholl and Calvine. With the spinning school in Dunkeld and Mrs Farquharson in Inver itself, there was no excuse for girls not to be well trained from an early age. There was the added advantage of also having local spinning wheel makers. John Farquharson in Inver and John Squires in Dunkeld , spinning wheel makers who were encouraged by the Duchess of Atholl, turned out improved models which enabled the spinners to increase their output. With the two flyer spinning wheel the Dowally women folk could produce four to eight hairs of yarn in a day and there is no reason to suppose that their Inver sisters were any less competent.

When the linen industry declined, Inver women had to look for other ways to bring in extra money although they continued to spin linen and wool yarn for domestic use for many years to come. As late as 1892 Beatrix Potter was photographing Maudie McDougall at her spinning wheel, although her aunt Helen Duff next door was a more competent spinner, being able to, 'spin the wheel like lightening'. [2] Miss Duff took a justifiable pride in her skill. 'I wad spin twelve cuts in aye dey an the hale I them wad dray through a weddin ring.' [3] The spinning wheel had belonged to Mrs Irvine, wife of the Reverend Alexander Irvine, minister of Little Dunkeld. Miss Duff's mother, a servant at the manse, would spin a web of handkerchiefs for the minister with a shade over her eyes on account of the fineness.

Beatrix also visited their former laundress, Kitty MacDonald, who lived at that time [1892] in the old boat house. The old lady produced a chemise which she and her mother had made from unbleached linen, spun by themselves and hand woven sixty years before and it was still in use. Beatrix put its durability down to the fact that it had not been weakened by chemicals used in bleaching. Stocks of such linen would last a family a lifetime.

With the arrival of the railway in Birnam in 1856, bringing with it the expansion of the tourist industry, opportunities for domestic service in the area increased. Inver girls had previously worked as servants in the better-off homes in Dunkeld and in the inns, but now the villas and lodging house keepers gave them employment. It was, of course, seasonal work which possibly explains the number of unemployed domestic servants listed in the census which was undertaken in April before the visitors had arrived. In addition, Inver women also catered for summer visitors in their homes.

Girls were content to do domestic work right up until the second world war. However, after the opportunities of more interesting work had opened out for women they were no longer prepared to accept the drudgery and low pay of domestic service. Inver housemaids had always been obliged to supplement the family income with casual work such as tending the forestry workers in the local bothy and at Ladywell, as well as working in the nurseries at Ladywell—mostly by gathering larch seed. There is a curious entry in the Atholl accounts of 1861 of payment to women working on the Embankment, at the time construction work on the Highland line was passing through Inver. Apart from that, the annual stint at the harvest and in the tattie fields helped to clothe the children the following winter.

The brighter Inver girls from the 1880s onwards were taken on as pupil teachers before going on to obtain their certificate. The above mentioned Maudie McDougall set herself up a teacher of piano. Mrs Scott also taught piano. There was always music in Inver—the Gow legacy.

1. H. Coates, *A Perthshire Naturalist* (London 1923), 21
2. L. Linder, *The Journal of Beatrix Potter 1881–1897* (London 1989), 297.
3. Ibid. 297

Mrs Irvine, wife of Rev. Alexander Irvine with her spinning wheel. [S Robertson]

Laundresses

From time immemorial and world wide, one of women's most fundamental tasks has been to keep the bed linen and body clothes of the family clean. In the eighteenth century, when houses were cramped, this chore was undertaken outside. This meant that in the winter months such work was impossible, so that a large supply of linen and underclothes was necessary. Household inventories bear this out. The weekly wash, so beloved of our grandmothers, was unheard of, except of course in the mansion houses fortunate enough to be equipped with a laundry.

The Medical Officer with the Duke of Cumberland's army gives us a vivid picture of the scene beside the River Ness in 1746:

> Their method of washing is by treading it in a tub with their naked feet, and holding at the same time their petticoats up to their middle ... they continue day after day, for they wash seldom and a great deal at a time. ... Those who are not worth a tub tread it in the river upon a large stone, under water for they seldom use soap. You will see in a warm morning the river edges lined with these sort of women, and frequently as many soldiers admiring their legs and thighs. [1]

Maggie Clark
at the slappie
by the River Tay.
[Dunkeld Archives]

Almost a hundred years later, in 1826, a visitor looked down from Telford's bridge and observed Dunkeld girls employing the same methods beside the Tay, but it is most probably that the Inver women undertook this task on the banks of the more accessible River Braan.

Kitty McDonald, Beatrix Potter's washer woman who lived out her last days in Inver, still employed traditional methods at Dalguise in the 1870s. In old age Beatrix recalled:

> The younger lasses trod the washing with their large white feet. I remember two dancing together in the one big wooden tub. Katie rubbed and scrubbed with her hands, wrinkled like a monkeys, but like her neighbours along the burn, she batted her clothes with a wooden thieval in the burn at the foot of the garden. [2]

Margaret Gow, faced with the daunting task of trying to keep eight children clean in a cottage smutty with peat smoke, must have felt she was fighting a losing battle with dirt. In addition, Niel, with his ever growing number of professional engagements, had to be decently turned out. His unvarying style of Highland dress of tartan trews, slatey blue waistcoat and jacket would be kept clean with fullers earth, while the white linen neckpiece usually worn by Scottish working men could be easily changed to preserve a clean appearance. Even as late as the 1860s, the white neck cloth or tucker was worn because thick garments were not washable, as related by Mary Wilson, pupil at the Duchess Anne School in Dunkeld:

> Every girl too, had to have something white at her neck, a clean tucker it was called. Some of us had little bands of plain linen, some had neat little strips of broiderie anglais. . . . Our dresses were mainly of thick stuff not washable, so I suppose the tuckers or collars were needed to keep our necks clean. [3]

Even into the early twentieth century, women were washing clothes by the riverside, as related by Mary Crerar in the same publication

> . . . washing of clothes was also done at the riverside, especially the widows who 'took in washing'. Fires were built on the river's bank above the Bridge, and enormous washings were done, dried in the gardens nearby, and dried at home. Other women had big mangles, and they regularly took in clothes to mangle. [4]

There were three such women working as laundresses in Inver in 1861. Elizabeth Laird, at the age of 38 was left a widow, a pauper, around 1850, with five children between two and sixteen years to fend for. Living in a two roomed cottage, there would be no possibility of taking in a lodger, so her obvious choice was to take in laundry. She had a shed erected near the smiddy, so no doubt she did her washing there where she could get a supply of water from the lade. A fire would be lit under a large tub and the clothes pounded with a theival until they were clean. If the weather was sunny, white items would be spread in the sun to be bleached. After the clothes were dried the business of starching and ironing was gone through. Goffering irons were used to iron the frills on cuffs and mutches. A poker would be made red hot in the fire and thrust into a socket in the iron, ready for use. Flat irons for other work were similarly heated. The clothes were finally aired and then packed in baskets, ready to be collected or delivered to the households. Mrs Laird's daughter Agnes attended the Duchess Anne school in

Dunkeld. By 1871 she had left home. The only remaining member of the family, William, was bringing in a wage as a nurseryman. A fellow nurseryman from Monzie shared a room with him as a lodger. By 1891 Elizabeth was living alone, described as an annuitant. Thereafter we loose sight of her.

Betty Macintosh was born in 1800, the daughter of Charles Macintosh, weaver and later musician. As a spinster and the only surviving daughter, her inevitable role in life was to look after and support her widowed mother. In the 1851 census the mother, aged 83, is described as a pauper and Betty is earning money by looking after a lodger, John Hogg, a sawmiller from Fife. Six years later the mother died leaving Betty on her own to fend for herself as a laundress. By this time the thatched cottage was becoming derelict and finally fell down in 1867. Thereafter she was housed in the Old Boat House which was a refuge for so many single women. In 1871 she was described in the rentals as a pauper, unable to pay any rent. She died shortly after, her whereabouts unknown, as she does not appear in the 1871 census which took place in April of that year. When Duchess Anne visited Inver in 1861 her comment on Betty Macintosh was, 'I cannot remember about the next cottage, which is occupied, I think by a young person and her mother'. [5] Facts wrong, who cared!

Duchess Anne took more of an interest in Catherine Stewart, our third laundress. She was left a widow in 1856 when her husband Charles broke his back in an accident at Birnam slate quarry. Miss Murray McGregor describes her as a little thick set woman with a dark upper lip. She occupied a one room cottage, a long low building attached to the old Boat House. Jane, her daughter, did the laundry work while Catherine had the support of her sons, Donald a blacksmith and Charles a woodcutter. Nothing more of her is known as she disappeared from the rentals around 1867.

As the village of Birnam developed washerwomen and laundresses tended to be centred there, near to the villas and lodging houses which they served. Women in Inver mostly undertook their own laundry. Those who were fortunate enough to have a boiler in an adjoining wash house were still carrying water from a spigot on the road and using flat irons heated at the fire. Those not so fortunate had to make do with heating a tub of water outside in their cabbage patch. There were some aids though. Zinc or glass wash boards were used to rub the clothes clean, while round tins of soft soap and bars of yellow soap aided the fight against dirt. Reckitts blue added to the rinsing water gave the whites a pristine appearance, while Robin's starch gave blouses, print dresses, napkins and handkerchiefs an added crispness.

By the early twentieth century Fisher's laundry from Aberfeldy were calling in the area and housewives, if they felt inclined, could relieve themselves of the chore of laundering sheets and bed-covers, although the spring time ritual of tramping blankets was still being practised until World War II. The arrival of a mains water supply and Hydro Board electricity made the weekly wash less laborious, as washing machines gradually made their appearance in the cottages of Inver. At first they were regarded with suspicion as older housewives were convinced that nothing could whiten cottons and linens like a wash in a boiler; but as easy care tablecloths and napkins and man-made fibres replaced the traditional materials, the wash tub was finally made redundant and wash boards became museum pieces.

1. *The Contrast or Scotland as it was in the year 1745* (Edinburgh and London 1825) Letter 8.
2. D. Rolland, *Beatrix Potter in Scotland* (London 1981)
3. E. Cox, ed. *Dunkeld Remembered* (Perth 1993) 45.
4. Ibid., 33
5. A.A. Bundle 893

Dressmakers

When Margaret Wiseman married Niel Gow around 1750 she would have been expected to bring to their home a good supply of bed linen and tablecloths as well as enough underwear to last her and her children, when they arrived. This was all to save her husband the expense of providing for her for many years to come. The household items were made from flax spun at home and given to the weaver to make into lengths. Underwear of harn, a courser flax, was made up the same way. Also spun by the family was yarn made from a mixture of wool and linen, woven into linsey—woolsey to be made up into dresses. All these items, except the dresses, were stitched by the lass herself. Later, throughout her married life, she would perform the same service for her husband and children. Dresses were made by itinerant dressmakers paid at the same rate as the tailors, according to Charlie Macintosh. [1] Old dresses were cut up to line the men folks' jackets or made down for children. Nothing could afford to be wasted.

By the end of the century the family presented a more prosperous appearance when turned out on a Sunday as the Reverend John Robertson notes in the *Old Statistical Account* of Little Dunkeld, 'Young men appear at church and market dressed in English cloth and round hats, and the young women in printed cottons or linens.' [2] Across the Tay at Dowally the minister reported, 'Then [in 1778] in short, the whole articles of dress of the people were home-made, excepting their bonnets, and a few shoes; now [in 1798] they are all bought from the merchants in Dunkeld.' [3]

Niel's daughter Margaret, who married James McDonald the Edinburgh dancing master, fared very differently from her mother. She would have been able to have her husband's shirts sewn by one of the many seamstresses plying their trade in the capital while her dresses would have been made by one of the city's mantua makers.

Following the completion of the Dunkeld bridge in 1809 more choice was open to the Inver women. They could either have the local weaver make up their own spun wool and linen yarn or they could make the trip across the bridge to Charles Blair or John Duff, merchants there, to purchase woollen cloth, muslin, lace, calico, printed cottons, pirns of thread and all the haberdashery requirements to make up their garments at home or to have them made to order in the shops. It was not until the 1861 census that Inver women are listed as Dressmakers, a more genteel type of employment than the laundress or domestic servant. By that time the Stewart Brothers had opened shops in both Dunkeld and Birnam with workrooms employing a number of dressmakers working full time. It was a highly skilled job for which the women had to undergo a long apprenticeship. Although there had been tentative attempts to invent a sewing machine since the turn of the century, seamstresses were still employed to do hand sewing. In the country districts, right up until the late 1920s, it was the practise of housewives to employ a dressmaker, working from her own home, for most everyday garments for themselves and their children while within many family circles there was an aunt who would obligingly make up materials bought cheaply in the shops, or work wonders with remaking hand-me-downs and even turning coats.

It was not until the 1930s that ready made clothes were within the price range of families fortunate enough to be in steady employment but World War II and clothing coupons challenged women of all sections of society to use their ingenuity to look smart. After the war, people longed for fashionable clothes at affordable prices. Dressmakers who had been through their rigorous apprenticeships and had worked miracles with remnants of material left over when the most attractive fabrics were being exported in the drive to earn dollars, found that there was no further demand for their services. Women who had tasted freedom in the three armed services were more attracted to the shop floor where the hours were shorter and the work less demanding in the new off the peg, serve yourself society. The village dressmaker, battling in her badly lit cottage, was a forgotten species. Let us remember two such in Inver and share their lives for a moment.

First, Isabella MacDonald. She was born in Inver in 1829, the only daughter of James MacDonald, one of the famous 'Clan' of cartwrights. Her mother died in 1831, the year she gave birth to her son James, leaving three motherless bairns. Their father James died in 1845 when Isabella was 16, leaving her to look after her grandmother and two brothers. After Granny's death in 1852 she and her brother James were left alone and she turned to dressmaking, possibly having had no formal training. If however, as was likely, she had attended Helen Farquharson's school nearby, she would have been an accomplished needle-woman.

Unfortunately we have no description of her appearance as she was out distributing tracts when the Duchess and Miss Murray McGregor called in 1861. Isabella was one of Inver's zealous women, no doubt being influenced by the pious Helen Farquharson. After the death of her brother James, Isabella was left on her own, still dressmaking. She died in 1905 in the house where she had been born 78 years before, the last of the 'Clan' whose skills had made its mark on the village for over a hundred years.

Elizabeth Clyde was born in Auchtergaven in 1813, the daughter of John Fleming who was in charge of the sawing operations at Inver sawmill in the 1830s. She married Clyde but was left a widow in poverty in Dundee. She sent her two children, John and Janet, to be brought up with their grandparents in Inver in the 1850s. John became a woodcutter under his grandfather but his sister Janet, aged 13, is cruelly described in the 1851 census as a pauper.

Elizabeth set up house with John and Janet in a two roomed cottage next door to the ruins of Niel Gow's house where she and her daughter plied their trade of dressmaking. Duchess Anne and Miss McGregor found her flustered when they announced their arrival in 1861. She had just got home 'having been as far as Perth'. 4

Her visitors described her as a tall woman with grey hair and Janet as a nice looking person. They remarked on 'the confusion of good furniture' and the Duchess was persuaded to rest in a very comfortable armchair. By this time son John was a skilled cabinet-maker. Elizabeth, like so many widows, ended her days in the Boat House Cottage, but not in poverty, when she died around 1882.

1. H Coates, *A Perthshire Naturalist* (London 1923), 21.
2. O.S.A. Vol XII 423
3. Ibid. 384
4. A.A. Bundle 893

The Howdie

> When I think of what I have come through in my profession, though it be one of the
> learned and the world not able to do without it, I have often thought that I could not
> wish waur on my deadliest enemy than a kittle case of midwifery, for surely it is a very
> obstetrical business, and far above a woman of common talons to practice. [1]

There was in every small community in the eighteenth century a woman who was knowledgable
and knew what had to be done in times of life's crises. Such a person was the midwife or howdie as
she saw people into the world and she saw them out of it. Although by the end of the eighteenth
century midwives were being trained in the hospitals of the main cities of Scotland, in the country
places she had no formal training. Her knowledge was acquired orally, passed on from the previous
generation, and her skills honed in the hard school of experience.

Life's most dramatic experiences of birth and death took place in the confines of the home and
girls learnt from an early age what lay ahead for them in childbirth as well as how to cope with the
death of their dear ones. There was no escaping reality. To ease the pain of such occasions there
were certain rituals to be observed, the celebratory 'merry meat' at birth and the wake at death.
Above all, the howdie had to be discreet, someone who could be trusted to keep sensitive knowledge
to herself. Ministers and elders were wont to pressurise the midwife to try to get the unfortunate
mother of an illegitimate child to divulge the father's name during the pain of her confinement.
The Inver folk at the turn of the eighteenth and nineteenth century were fortunate to have such a
one in the person of Janet Low, husband of Peter who was an estate worker and next door neighbour
to Elizabeth Borrie.

Charles Macintosh remembers her as a tall, wiry woman, strong minded, possibly held in some
awe by the children of the village. They would see a man on horseback arrive at the cottage door,
from which she would quickly emerge with a bag in her hand, get on the horse behind the anxious
rider and off they would gallop. The young women of the village would look on her with some
curiosity and respect, wondering when their turn would come to make use of her services. And the
old folk and the sick knew that when their time came, she would be there to do what she could to
ease their pain and see them out of this world as she had ushered their children into it. Along with
a few of the other women of the village, she was well versed in the Bible and was wont to quote
scripture and argue the finer doctrinal points of such weighty matters are predestination. Janet
herself had a family and knew the pain of parting with a son to America, never to see him again.
The letters between father and son reveal a loving, close family, proud of their son John's
achievements in the New World. Forever mindful of his spiritual needs, his mother quotes in the
next family letter the text of that day's sermon preached in Little Dunkeld church. Truly a woman of
high principal.

Throughout the nineteenth century and well into the twentieth century, home confinements
were the norm unless there were complications in which case the mother could be taken into Perth
Royal Infirmary. The expectant mother would engage a nurse privately, who would take up
residence in the home and, under the supervision of the doctor, deliver the baby.

By this time the pains of childbirth were relieved by the use of anaesthesia pioneered by Sir James Simpson while the work of Joseph Lister in the use of carbolic acid reduced the loss of life through infection. Queen Victoria was one of the beneficiaries of these improvements when she produced her eighth child. So concerned was she at the plight of women in childbirth in rural areas that, as part of the celebration of her Golden Jubilee in 1887, she set up a scheme to supply trained district nurses who worked under the supervision of local committees. The money had been raised by women donating to the Women's Jubilee Offering.

The Dunkeld and Birnam District Nursing Association was inaugurated in 1902 under the leadership of Mrs Arthur Harris. Two nurses, occupying a nurses cottage in Little Dunkeld conveniently near the Lagmor doctors surgery, were responsible for an incredibly wide area stretching out to Amulree, Spitalfield, Dowally and Dalguise. This they covered by bicycle until a Morris Cowley car was purchased for them around 1929. By that time they were involved in home visits to attend to the seriously ill as well as minor accidents, ante natal and post natal work and school inspections. From the point of view of national health, the importance of district nurses' maternity and child welfare work could hardly be over estimated. The scheme was financed by local subscription, five hundred households in the district contributing sums ranging from twenty pounds to two shillings per annum, collected by volunteers. Gifts of old linen, clothing, nursery accessories, even fruit, flowers and magazines were donated. Fund raising activities ranged from fifteen pounds realised by a jumble sale in Little Dunkeld to one hundred and fifty two pounds raised by a garden fete organised by Mrs Cox of Dungarthill, who retired in 1929 after giving twenty three years service to the association. This excellent service, given by successive dedicated nurses and voluntary workers, was taken over by the National Health service in 1945. There were still district nurses in the nurses home in Little Dunkeld until 1990, under the direction of the National Health Service.

By the 1930s it was becoming the practice to go to hospital to have ones baby, although a home delivery was still an option. Inver women had the choice of Aberfeldy Cottage Hospital, Meiklour Maternity Hospital or Perth Royal Infirmary. For those who could afford it, St Johnstone's Private Nursing Home in Perth was an option. Nowadays home deliveries are discouraged and women must go to Perth Royal Infirmary provided that a bed is available. Failing that, they must travel the further twenty two miles to Ninewells Hospital in Dundee. So much for progress! Despite the difficulties of location, women today may be thankful for a health service which gives them the likely expectation of a safe delivery of their babies.

Erica Lyon, who now occupies Niel Gow's cottage in Inver, is a retired midwife, successor, two centuries on, to Janet Low the howdie. Margaret Gow, who presented Niel with five sons and three daughters between the years 1751 and 1765, died, presumably worn out with the effort, a couple of years after the birth of Daniel, her youngest son. She could have benefited from Erica's expert administration.

It is a matter of regret that neither Niel nor any of his sons composed a tribute to the first Margaret, although the second Margaret, when she died, inspired Niel's most moving tribute to her in his 'Lament on the Death of his Second Wife' and Nathaniel celebrated her in his composition 'In Praise of Stepmothers'.

1.   J. Galt, *The Howdie and other tales* (Edinburgh 1923), 25

Published sources:

Mary Ann Allburger, *Scottish fiddlers and their music* (London 1983)

J. Anderson, *Chronicles of the Atholl and Tullibardine Families VI* (Aberdeen 1991)

R.L. Brown ed., *Robert Burn's Tour of the Highlands and Stirlingshire 1787* (Edinburgh 1973)

Frederick Teague Carswick, *Inscriptions from the remaining stones of St James's Pentonville Road, Clerkenwell* 1884.

Robert Chalmers, *The Thrieplands of Fingask* (London 1880)

Henry Coates, *A Perthshire Naturalist* (London 1923)

The Contrast or Scotland as it was in 1745 (Edinburgh & London 1825)

E. Cox, ed., *Dunkeld Remembered* (Dunkeld 1993)

Henry Dryerre, *Blairgowrie, Stormont and Strathmore Worthies* (Edinburgh 1903)

Right Rev. Robert Forbes (ed. Rev. J.B. Craven), *Journal of Episcopal Visitations 1762–1770* (London 1886)

Dr Garnet, *Observations of a Tour through the Highlands and part of the Western Isles of Scotland* (London 1800)

Maxtone Graham, *The beautiful Mrs Graham* (London 1927)

Maxtone Graham, *The Oliphants of Gask* (London 1910)

Elizabeth Grant of Rothiemurchus, *Memoirs of a Highland Lady* (Edinburgh 1988)

A.R.B. Haldane, *New ways through the glens* (Newton Abbot 1973)

'Jenny Horne', *Idylls and sketches of Dalmachair* (Dingwall 1931)

R. Leitch, *The book of Sandy Stewart* (Edinburgh 1988)

L. Linder, *The Journal of Beatrix Potter 1881–1897* (London 1989)

Rev. James Robertson General, *View of the Agriculture in the County of Perth* (Perth 1831)

Joseph McGregor, *Memoir of Niel Gow in a Collection of Reels and Strathspeys.* (Edinburgh 1837).

F. Marian McNeill, *The Scots cellar* (Edinburgh 1956)

Sir Alexander Muir Mackenzie of Delvine, ed., *Tacketies and tyres in Strathbraan* (Perth, 1908)

Alexander G. Murdoch, *The Fiddler in Scotland* (London 1888)

Old Statistical Account Vol XII (1798)

Deborah Rolland, *Beatrix Potter in Scotland* (London 1981)

Keith Sanger & Alison Kinnaird, *Tree of strings* (Musselburgh 1992)

John Shaw, *Water power in Scotland*

D. Stewart of Garth, *Sketches of the Highlanders of Scotland I* (Inverness 1885)

J. Stewart Murray, 7th Duke of Atholl, *Chronicles of the Atholl and Tullibardine Families I–V* (Edinburgh 1895–1908)

Journals and newspapers:

People's Journal
Perthshire Advertiser
Chambers Edinburgh Journal 1844
Scots Magazine 1809
Robert Scott Fittis, *Miscellanea Perthensis 1853–1861* (newspaper cuttings)

Unpublished sources:

Atholl Archives Rentals and estate papers.
1479 Duchess Anne's notes on 'Blair District 1860–1861
Minutes of the Highland Society of London.
Ph.D. thesis by David Mackie, 1999.

Index

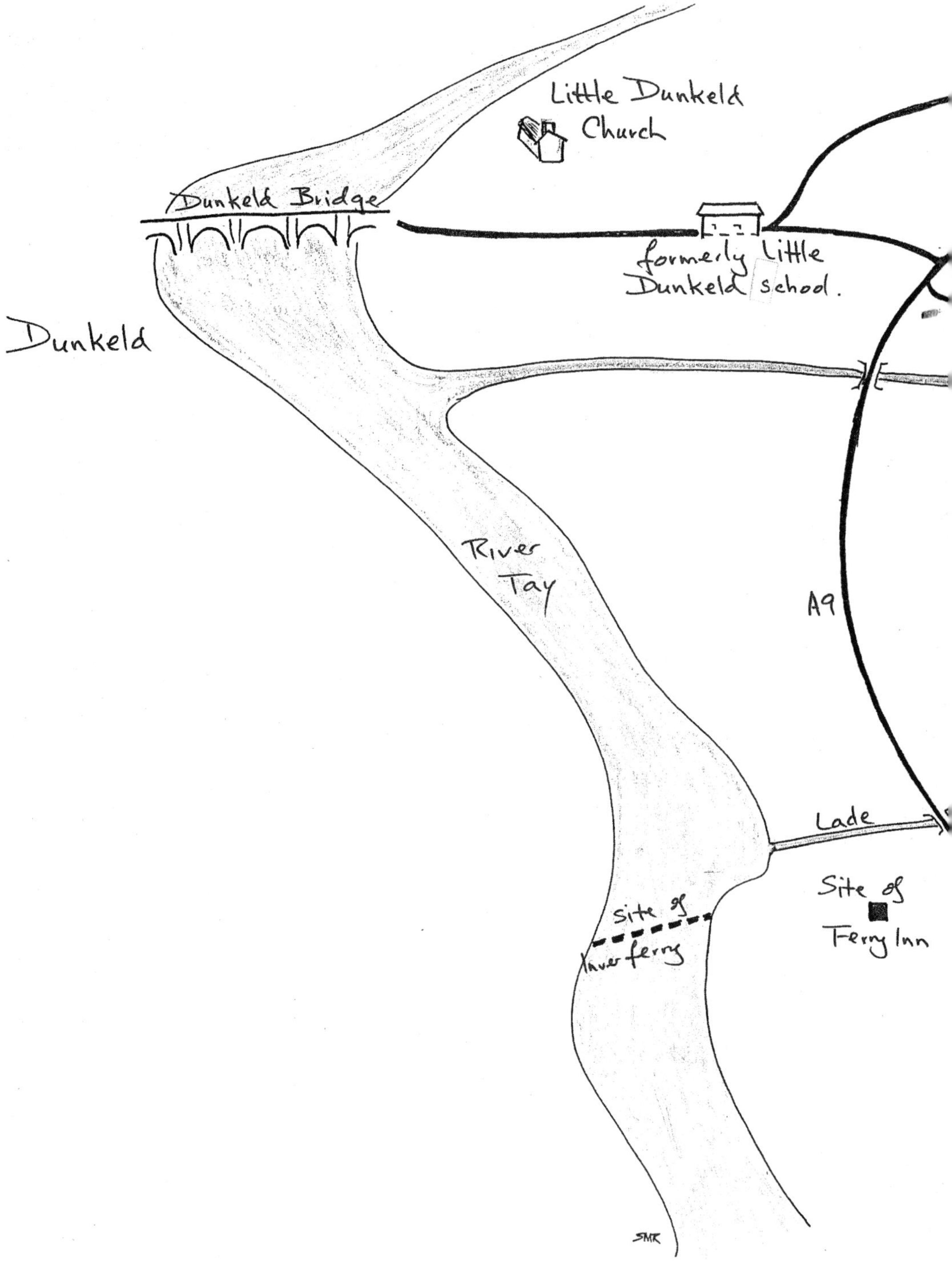

Little Dunkeld
Church

Dunkeld Bridge

Dunkeld

formerly Little
Dunkeld school.

River
Tay

A9

Lade

site of
river ferry

Site of
Ferry Inn

SMR

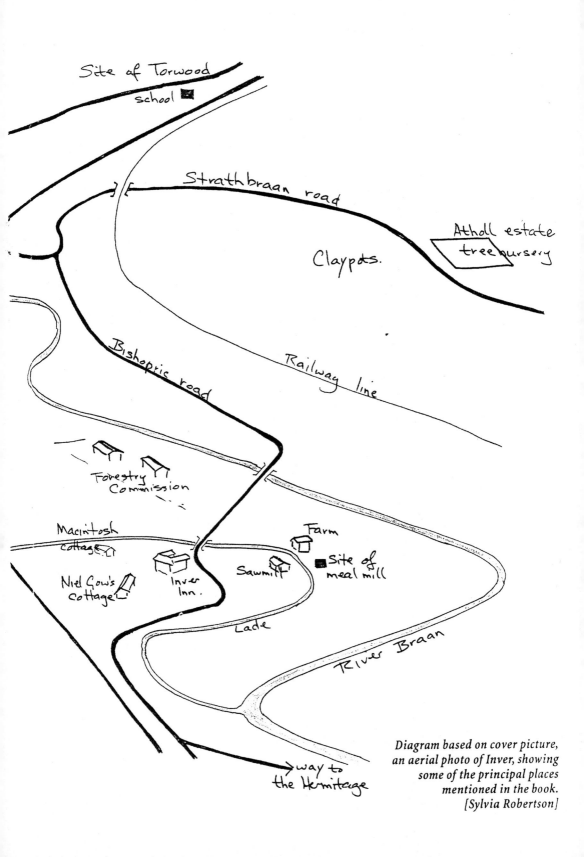

Diagram based on cover picture,
an aerial photo of Inver, showing
some of the principal places
mentioned in the book.
[Sylvia Robertson]